GOLF BETWEEN THE WARS

'Golf is a science, the study of a lifetime, in which you may exhaust yourself, but never your subject. It is a contest, a duel, or a mêlée, calling for courage, skill, strategy and self-control. It is a test of temper, a trial of honour, a revealer of character. It affords a chance to play the man and act the gentleman. It means going into God's out-of-doors, getting close to nature, fresh air, exercise, a sweeping-away of mental cobwebs, genuine recreation of tired tissues. It includes companionship with friends, social intercourse, opportunities for courtesy, kindliness, and generosity to an opponent. It promotes not only physical health, but moral force.'

David R. Forgan

Golf Between The Ears

Bill Raymond
and
Rodney Werninck

B T E Publishing

© Bill Raymond and Rodney Werninck 2001

First published in 2001 by
BTE Publishing
PO Box 3847
Blandford Forum
Dorset

www.golfbte.co.uk
BTEpublishing@aol.com

British Library Cataloguing in Publication Data.
A Catalogue record for this book is available
from the British Library.

ISBN 1-90424-700-8

All characters in this book are fictitious.
Any similarity to persons living or dead is purely coincidental.

Typeset in Dante 12 on 15 by
Carnegie Publishing
Carnegie House
Chatsworth Road
Lancaster
www.carnegiepub.co.uk
www.wooof.net

Printed and bound by Bookcraft, Midsomer Norton

The Authors

Bill Raymond

Bill started playing golf at an early age, becoming a scratch golfer at 19. His first significant encounter with the mental problems posed by golf came in the Amateur Championship at Troon in 1968, when he missed a straight uphill yard putt to beat his fancied opponent. As he recalls: 'It was the first time I had thought about an action that before had been purely automatic. What a disaster! I felt totally demoralised.'

Since that day Bill has studied the mental challenge of the game and, as no instructional books were available on the subject, he set about devising his own techniques for coping. These helped him to maintain his scratch handicap for nearly 30 years and represent his native country, Scotland. A meeting with his co-author Rodney at a golf event last year persuaded Bill that a simple guide to the mental skills required for golf was possible and *Golf Between the Ears* began to take shape.

As Bill explains: 'If *Golf Between the Ears* had been available to me back in 1968, I am convinced I would have become a better, more consistent player. I hope that it helps many, many golfers to improve their game and get more fun and enjoyment out of their golf.'

Rodney Werninck

A keen sportsman, Rodney has always been fascinated by how his performance could vary so much at different times. He saw it not just in himself, but also in others he competed against in his favourite sports of judo, squash and sailing. This interest has stayed with him and, in business, he was a keen student of the psychology of performance and human interaction.

This deep fascination led Rodney to train as a cognitive behavioural therapist and specialise in dealing with individuals suffering from anxiety and stress-related problems. He was particularly interested to see how the way someone thinks about things can affect their performance, whether on a stage, in business or in the sporting arena. After further research, it became clear to Rodney that good thinking skills could enhance sporting performance. As a teacher of these skills he was convinced that not only golfers, but *all* sportsmen would benefit from an instructional guide along the lines of *Golf Between the Ears*.

Having only taken up golf seriously in the last few years, Rodney is beginning to discover that a good mental approach is more important in golf than any other game!

Contents

Introduction

'Golf is a game played between your two ears' - Anon

Have you ever wished that you could play a round of golf without your concentration being disturbed or being put off by someone or something? If so, this is the book for you! We can't, of course, guarantee that nothing will ever put you off again after reading this book. However, if you can put into practice some of the simple techniques we suggest, we are confident you will be much better equipped to deal with the 'mental hazards' encountered during a round of golf.

There is no other sport quite like golf for testing the player's mental abilities. The time spent actually engaged in 'golfing' or swinging the club is miniscule, perhaps three to four minutes out of several hundred minutes spent on the course! That leaves plenty of time for the mind to wander into unwanted areas. Loss of confidence, self-criticism, pessimism, anger, and more, can be the result.

These 'mental hazards' are very familiar to us all. Such things as:

First tee nerves

The little prayer hoping that you will get a good one away... 'All those people are watching me...'

Gamesmanship

Opponents rattling their change... The little remark about your swing...

Distractions

People chattering...Thinking about work...

Disasters waiting to happen

'I never play this hole well...' 'This good golf can't last...'

Pressure shots

'This is vital...' 'Must hole this...' Simple shots suddenly become extremely difficult.

The list is endless and, as we all know, these situations usually result in bad shots and the ruination of a good round. These mental hazards are very real, presenting as much of a challenge to golfers as the physical hazards on the course. The big question is, can these hazards be overcome, and if so, how?

Numerous books have been written on the role of the mind in golf. Many of these have been psychological studies giving much more information than the average golfer can cope with or, for that matter, readily understand. Most golfers are unwilling to go into the matter in such depth. They want straightforward answers to their personal mental obstacles without wading through too much technical stuff to construct their own solutions. 'Analysis can lead to paralysis' as they say!

To make the whole subject more accessible and to help put it in an easily understood format, we went out and talked to club golfers. We asked them to tell us what mental problems they were encountering. We invited them to explain what went on in their mind at these critical times and how it adversely affected their game.

From this research we have put together a collection of scenarios which take place at a mythical club called Dizzy Heights. Amongst the fictitious golfers who play there we will all recognise some part of our own golfing character. There's Steve, who's afraid of short putts; Jim who is put off by the slightest noise; and Lucy who just knows that her medal round is going to end in disaster. Many more characters fill the pages with a wide spectrum of mental problems. You will recognise many of them and also identify with some of them!

Amongst these stories will be something which every golfer can relate to. 'Oh yes, that's exactly what happened to me' was the standard reply when we showed the scenarios to a sample of golfers. Hopefully you will find your own personal mental obstacle in the Dizzy Heights Casebook. For each of the cases there is a brief assessment of what the mental problem is plus some straightforward advice about how to overcome it.

The style of this book is a friendly, light-hearted approach to a complex subject. We want reading it to be an enjoyable and informative experience, not a serious study of the darkest recesses of your golfing mind!

Our aim was to create a no nonsense guide to handling the mental obstacles for which golf is notorious and so improve your game. We hope you find it useful and that *Golf Between the Ears* will become a trusted friend throughout your golfing career.

Bill Raymond
Rodney Werninck

Foreword (1)

Golf is the greatest game in the world! I should know, having been involved in it all my life. Golf is a sociable sport providing the opportunity to enjoy a challenge in pleasant surroundings. What more could we wish from our favourite game? Well, I suppose many golfers would say – 'If you could take away the fear of failure and the mental pressure this can create, then the game would be perfect!'

Yes, golf is frustrating and that is what makes it such a fascinating and compelling game. Just when you think you are in the groove, everything goes haywire and you are struggling to play anywhere near your handicap! Throughout my years in the game I have seen many competent players who are capable of hitting all the shots, unable to play anywhere near their potential due to the tricks that the mind can play. Professionals and amateurs alike can fall victim to these mental hazards.

Numerous books have been written on the mental side of golf, but *Golf Between The Ears* tackles this difficult subject in a completely original way. Using an easy to understand format that includes solving actual problems, it gives a clear insight into how we can help ourselves. I am sure that golfers everywhere will appreciate its straightforward approach to a complex problem. There is something useful in it for every golfer who wants to improve his mental skills.

I hope that you find some of the answers you seek amongst these pages. The golfer who masters the mind game is a formidable opponent indeed!

Jim Christine
Member of the Golf International Teaching Panel
Member of the Ryder Cup Limited Board
Member of the PGA Board
Professional, Worplesdon Golf Club

Foreword (2)

I was delighted to be asked to write an introduction to Golf Between the Ears as I have always felt that the mental side of golf is something that is often neglected by teachers and players.

Golfers of all standards, from the top professionals to the high handicapper, can have their game totally destroyed by 'Little gremlins' playing tricks in their mind. For the average club golfer these problems usually reveal themselves in such statements as 'I always play that 18th hole badly', 'I can't hit a shot if there are people watching me' and 'I get nervous when I have a good score going'. Whilst for top players who lose form, the problems are usually centred around 'self doubt', 'fear of failure' or 'loss of confidence'. In both cases nothing has really fundamentally gone wrong with their technique but their mind is preventing them from playing to their full potential.

Most golfers put up with these problems and accept them as part of the game, not realising that the skills for overcoming the mental challenge can be learned just like a good swing technique. I have played with and taught many fine golfers who could have achieved much greater success if they had been willing to spend some time in learning to play a better game 'Between the Ears'. Unfortunately the mental side of golf has never been easy to explain or understand!

Golf Between the Ears meets this need admirably, having been specifically designed to simplify the learning of mental skills and to present the subject in an easily understood and amusing way. The case studies I am sure will strike a chord with golfers everywhere!

Foreword (2)

I am certain that any golfer who wants to improve his or her game will benefit from reading this book. There is definitely something in it for every golfer – including myself! It is never too late to learn . . .

Doug Sewell

Surrey Amateur Champion	1956/58
England Home International Team	1956–60
Walker Cup	1957/59
English Amateur Stroke Play Champion	1957/59
English Amateur Champion	1958/60
Sunningdale Foursomes	1959
Commonwealth Team	1959
Eisenhower Trophy	1960
Golf Illustrated Gold Vase	1960
Surrey Open	1964
Wentworth Pro/Am Foursomes	1968
West of England Open Professional Championship	1968/70
Winner (tied) Martini International	1970
Runner Up Penfold Tournament	1971/73
Club Professional Champion	1973/75
Mini Ryder Cup Team	1973–75

OPENING THOUGHTS

– The mental side of golf is nothing new –
– They say golf is 50% mental –
– Playing closer to your potential –
– Golf is a bit like life… –
– Golf is fun –
– Using this book –
– The mental skills needed for golf –

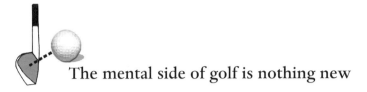

The mental side of golf is nothing new

Nearly a hundred years ago, the six times Open Champion Harry Vardon recognised the importance of the mental side of the game in his instructional book *The Complete Golfer*. His tips included:

> *'Always make up your mind definitely and finally before taking up your stance what club you are going to use and exactly the kind of shot you want to play with it. When you have taken up your position, but still ponder in a state of uncertainty, it is very probable that your mind will be affected by your hesitation, and then your swing and the result thereof will be bad.'*

> *'At the beginning of a match do not worry yourself with the idea that the result is likely to be against you. By reflecting thus upon the possibilities of defeat one often becomes too anxious and loses one's freedom of style.'*

Psychology and golf have moved on a long way since Harry Vardon gave these simple pieces of advice. Today, most of the top players seek help with the mental side of their game, using a sports psychologist just as often as a teaching guru. Technically, the world stars are excellent, but they recognise that the mental hazards of the game can easily disrupt their finely tuned swings and cause poor shots. The stars of today know that improving their mental approach to the game will bring them better results. We believe this is equally true for the club golfer.

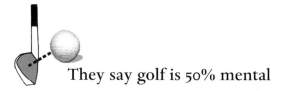

They say golf is 50% mental

The average player who wants to improve his game usually grabs a bucket of balls and heads for the practice ground, or books some lessons with the professional. He or she rarely considers spending time working on their mental game. The phrases 'Golf is 50% mental' and 'It's all between the ears' are frequently heard around the clubhouse, but how often do we hear a discussion about the techniques for improving that 'half' of the game?

Anyone who has played golf soon realises that their thought processes play a big part in determining how well they play. Beginners quickly learn golf's oldest excuse: 'I was put off by . . .' and rapidly collect a long list of reasons to explain why they are not playing as well as they can. These excuses normally involve something over which they appear to have no control!

Golfers will use excuses such as 'Too many things on my mind', 'I'm not in the right frame of mind', and 'My mind wasn't on it today'. Unfortunately, these responses to poor play are frequently accepted as facts as if they are out of the player's control. Many golfers seem willing to put up with these mind problems because they have never considered the possibility that they can be tackled just like flaws in their swing.

The mental game can be a very personal thing. It is something that involves our inner self and recognising our own strengths and weaknesses. Even if we could afford a personal mind guru to help, not many of us would take the time to visit one and discuss our golfing problems. Most of us wishing to improve this side of our game would probably prefer to try and glean some hints from a self-help book like this.

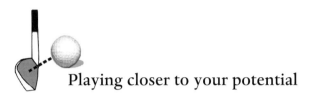

Playing closer to your potential

Our aim in writing this book is to help you play more consistently by avoiding the destructive effects of the mind on your swing and your scoring. It is not a book about technique, but a guide to helping you overcome the problem of your mind interfering with your natural ability to perform.

Most people are unable to put in the extra time required to improve their technique or the physical side of their game. Building what the professional tells them into their swing usually involves many hours on the practice ground, and less time on the course. However, we are convinced that every golfer can improve their game by working on their mental approach.

Golf enjoys worldwide popularity because it allows even the worst player the chance to hit a shot as good as the top pros. He or she can even enjoy doing that on the same stage! We have all holed a good putt or hit a spanking drive whilst playing a famous course and thought vainly to ourselves… *Nicklaus couldn't have done much better.* However, the trick, of course, is consistency. We don't hit our good shots or play our best golf all the time, otherwise we would be on tour!

Although their technique might not be very sound, most club golfers could improve their consistency by preventing their mind from interfering with their own rhythm and swing. If they could reduce the disastrous effects of such things as pressure, gamesmanship, distractions, self doubt, etc. on their game, then they will surely play nearer their best more often.

Gaining control of your thought processes will help prevent your mind interfering with your swing and causing needless bad shots. Mastering some of the basic mental skills discussed in the following chapter will allow you to see the game in a different light. Your enjoyment of the game will also be increased as you begin to take control of situations you previously feared.

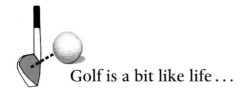 ## Golf is a bit like life...

No other game winkles out all the weaknesses in our character like golf does. The ups and downs of a round of golf are like the swings and roundabouts of life – the golfer's mood at any point in time being determined by how well or badly the round is going.

The situations and pressures our mind is expected to handle on the golf course are very similar to those we encounter at work and in our personal lives. However, there is one major difference: with golf you cannot hide from your mistakes! Golfers are responsible for every shot they take and their total is posted against their name at the end of the round.

In some ways, golf produces more challenges than life. The golfer is under constant pressure to perform in full view of everyone and take full responsibility for his or her actions. Imagine if every time you made a mistake at work the boss displayed a poster detailing what you had done! Or when you had a family argument, a note of what happened was distributed to your neighbours!

A golfer can cite all sorts of reasons for playing poorly, but in the end he or she must recognise that they have only themselves to blame for a bad round. Conversely, of course, they can take all the credit for a winning score! A golfer has to stand up and be counted for his or her performance. There is no hiding place, certainly not in the mind.

The skills a golfer needs to overcome the mental hazards posed by the game will also prove useful in everyday life. If you can learn to handle the pressures of golf, then you can just about cope with anything that life will throw at you!

Golf is fun ...

At the end of the eighteenth century, Tobias Smollet described the game as it was then played around Edinburgh: *'On the fields called the Links the players divert themselves at a game called Golf using a curious kind of bat tipped with horn, and small elastic balls of leather, stuffed with feathers.'*

Several hundred years later, although the technology has changed somewhat, the enthusiasm and passion of golfers has not diminished. In fact, it has spread across the globe. There are now very few countries where golf is not played. The only thing that can compare with the enduring passion to play golf is the equally strong desire to talk about it! Golfers are never lost for words when it comes to talking golf. There is always something to analyse, recount, and laugh at.

This has been the inspiration for many famous authors who have been moved to pen their thoughts on golfers and their foibles. More humorous stories have surely been written about golf than any other sport. Some of our favourite authors include the acknowledged master P.G. Wodehouse and Patrick Campbell, who showed such marvellous insight into the golfing mind in his hilarious book *How to Become a Scratch Golfer.*

This ability of golfers to laugh at themselves is one of the best antidotes to the mental problems created by the game. We now know that the simple act of laughing can stimulate the body's immune system, our inbuilt defence system against disease. By lowering stress and tension, laughter can help reduce the chances of heart attacks and strokes. Poking fun at yourself and your failings can also be useful in developing self confidence and self awareness.

So remember that golf is for 'playing at' and not for 'working at'. If we can keep our approach to the game from becoming too serious, our performance will benefit. We will be able to cope more easily with the bad bounces and the putts that lip out, whilst some humour will also ease tension and improve our mood during the round.

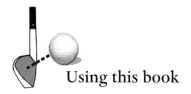 **Using this book**

The aim of this book is to provide you with a straightforward guide to the techniques which can be used to overcome golf's mental hazards. To achieve this we went out and asked club golfers their views about such a book. The most frequent comments we heard were:

'Please make it easy to read and understand. Keep it simple.'

'Most books on golfing psychology are far too complex; they tell you what's going wrong but not how to correct it.'

'My problem never seems to be covered . . .'

We therefore set out to try and meet the above requirements by basing the book on two main sections:

1. THE BASIC MENTAL SKILLS

A simple guide to the basic mental skills required for golf with clear explanations of how to learn these skills.

2. THE DIZZY HEIGHTS CASEBOOK

A collection of golfing scenarios featuring many of the mental problems encountered on the course. These are based on real life experiences related to us by golfers of all abilities. Amongst them you will most likely find some of your own mental golfing hazards. Each problem is then discussed with reference to The Basic Mental Skills section and suggestions given as to how that problem can best be overcome.

So you can either begin by jumping straight into 'The Dizzy Heights Casebook' and see if the golfers there are experiencing the same problems as yourself. Or you can gain an understanding of the basic skills, and then move on to the Casebook and see how these can be applied to everyday golfing situations. We don't envisage anyone learning and applying all the techniques outlined in the book. However, we are sure that golfers of **all** abilities will find something useful, a technique or an idea which will help them improve the mental side of their game.

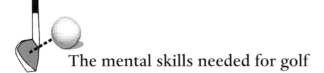

The mental skills needed for golf

Many of the mental obstacles which beset golfers and affect their performance arise from conditions that cause anxiety. These are normally a fear of looking foolish or failing, a fear of being humiliated, and the fear of competition and the pressures it brings. Being intimidated by 'better' or 'more confident' players can also create anxiety through feeling 'inadequate' and inwardly angry. Attitudinal problems are the other main cause of mental problems for golfers. These usually take the form of 'lack of confidence', 'unnecessary aggression', 'poor concentration', and 'lack of assertiveness'.

To meet and overcome this wide range of mental difficulties requires a number of new thinking skills. These we have called the Basic Mental Skills. We have studied the various techniques used by cognitive therapists – techniques that have been tried and tested in various sport settings, and simplified these into six basic skills:

- ❑ Staying relaxed
- ❑ Getting your thinking right
- ❑ Goal setting
- ❑ Focusing your thoughts
- ❑ Taking responsibility
- ❑ Building confidence

In the next section we will try and make these proven techniques easily understood and applied, by avoiding confusing terminology and keeping the message as clear and simple as possible. It won't all apply to you, but we are certain that every golfer will find something within these pages that will help them overcome one or more of their own mental obstacles.

THE BASIC MENTAL SKILLS

– Staying relaxed is vital –
– Getting your thinking right –
– Goal setting –
– Focusing your thoughts –
– Taking responsibility –
– Building confidence –

1   STAYING RELAXED IS VITAL

The relationship between the degree of physical activation, in other words getting yourself 'uptight' or
'keyed up', and sporting performance, is well docu-
mented. As you can see from the graph below, as physical activation
increases so sporting performance increases until an 'optimum' point is
reached where the level of physical activation is just right for the task. If

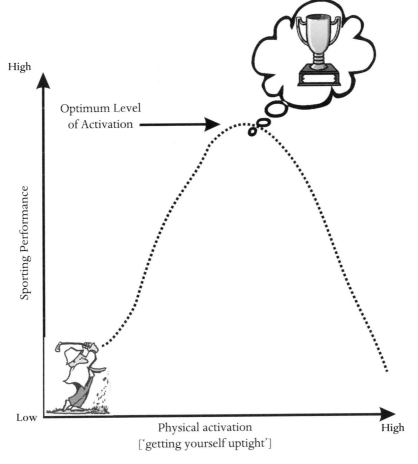

the level of physical activation continues to increase, then it becomes too much for the task, and sporting performance decreases.

A degree of physical activation is necessary for even straightforward tasks. We need it to even get out of bed first thing in the morning, heave our golf clubs into the back of the car and walk round the golf course! However, it is important to bear in mind that different tasks need different levels of physical activation.

Sports, like weightlifting or shot putting, require huge amounts of explosive energy which are generated from very high levels of physical activation. You may have seen these types of athletes furiously 'psyching' themselves up for a competition. On the other hand, golf requires very precise movements of the body and very accurate hand to eye co-ordination.

After a considerable amount of practice, the mind and body learn to work together to perform the highly complex tasks needed to play golf well. These can range from a full-blooded 300 yard drive to a delicate chip over a bunker. The millions of micro adjustments that the body needs to make for a good golf shot eventually become automatic. This process is similar to learning to drive a car. Fairly quickly we don't have to think consciously how to depress the clutch in order to change gear smoothly. Once these skills have been learned through repetition, we know that it is best to leave them alone to get on with the job and to not consciously interfere with the process.

Since the complex tasks involved in playing golf require very accurate control of the muscles, we perform them best when we are reasonably relaxed – in other words, when we have a relatively low level of physical activation. Stress and tension in the body can interfere with our performance. Have you ever noticed how when you are feeling relaxed and not under pressure that you usually hit more of your good shots? And yet when you get out there on that first tee in a competition with everyone watching, a good shot seems a remote possibility!

This stress and tension or physical activation usually occurs as a result of being too excited or anxious. Not only does over activation interfere with your natural ability to play a good shot but it tends to make you more easily distracted. Thus controlling the level of physical activation and staying cool, calm and collected on the golf course will help you play to the best of your ability.

Learning to relax on the course

To achieve your optimum level of physical activation, you need to control both the level of physical stimulation and tension in your body as well as the anxiety and negative thoughts that pass through your mind. The mind skills necessary for dealing with anxiety and negative thoughts are dealt with in the next section entitled 'Getting your Thinking Right' on page 20.

Relaxing and lowering physical activation when you are under pressure is a skill that must be learned and practised, initially, away from the golf course. Clearly, when you are faced with an important shot, you do not have very long to relax and reduce the tension in your body. You must therefore learn to induce the relaxation response quickly. Practising for fifteen or twenty minutes, three or four times a week, for several weeks should allow you to bring about a relaxation response within a few minutes on the golf course. An effective relaxation technique or 'trigger' should include:

◻ **muscle relaxation**
◻ **a mental device** (i.e. a word, phrase, or process used to shift attention inward)
◻ **imagery** (using mental pictures of pleasant and relaxing places).

After frequent practising of the relaxation technique, the mental device and the imagery become strongly associated with a feeling of relaxation. This means that when you are in a stressful situation on the golf course, you can bring the mental device and imagery to mind allowing the associated relaxation response to follow and help reduce the tension.

Creating your own relaxation 'trigger'

Relaxation techniques may be learned at classes, from books or relaxation tapes. Many sportsmen and women even take up yoga or Tai-chi. If none of these appeal, then we have put together a simple relaxation method that you can do on your own at home. All you need to create your own instant relaxation technique is detailed in the Appendix at the back of this book.

Make your own Instant Relax Trigger... Turn to page 139

Part of the technique is deep muscle relaxation when you repeat the word '**calm**' in your mind as you breathe out. Once you have practised this many times you will associate the easy breathing and repeating '**calm**' with muscle relaxation. Then, just repeating '**calm**' for a few minutes will become the 'trigger' for your muscles to relax, even on the golf course! Alternatively you could use your relaxing image as the 'trigger'.

Once you have your own relaxation 'trigger', you can use it on the course to help reduce tension and induce a feeling of calm. Just think how useful that could be!

Imagine you are in a tight match and you are facing a vital putt. You begin to feel anxious, your muscles tighten up, your mind begins to race – you need to calm down! Your relaxation 'trigger' will do just that, helping to reduce your level of physical activation and so making you better prepared to play the shot well. So start work now making your own 'trigger' and see how useful this can be in improving your golf. It takes some practice but it's worth it!

Don't forget the physical side

One of the many attractions of golf is that you do not have to be very athletic, strong or fit to enjoy the game. Nonetheless, keeping yourself as active, fit and healthy as possible will help you to enjoy this game even more, as well as making you more resilient to tension. You may have noticed that when you are tired and perhaps your body is aching, you are more prone to frustration and more liable to make mistakes.

It is therefore worth learning to pay attention to the tension coming from your body. Look for tension or a cramped feeling in areas of the body such as the hands and forearms, shoulders, thighs, etc. Obstructive tension in your muscles not only affects performance but can cause or aggravate injury. Tensing and then slowly relaxing those muscles several times and gently shaking your limbs may relieve this. Also use your relaxation technique to keep such tension at bay.

Golf requires a comparatively low state of physical activation. Make sure you thoroughly learn and practise a relaxation technique or 'trigger', which will rapidly help to reduce tension in your body at more or less any time during a round of golf.

Remember you have the best chance of playing well when you are at the optimal level of physical activation. By using your relaxation 'trigger' you will attain that optimal level.

2   GETTING YOUR THINKING RIGHT

The human mind is the most complex tool in the known universe. Unfortunately, the instruction manual seems to have got lost! The way we think about things, our views and attitudes have all mainly developed as a result of the experiences we have had during our lives and the way we dealt with them. As a result we assume that our thoughts and attitudes are correct and are the only views to hold in any particular situation. However, the good news is that even though the 'grey matter' between our ears may be the source of mental obstacles on the golf course, therein also lies the solution! Just as we can learn to improve our golf technique, we can also learn effective new thinking skills that can enhance our performance on the course.

From the large body of research carried out in recent years, we know that worry and apprehension associated with a state of anxiety are a major hindrance to sporting performance. As the levels of worry and anxiety rise the sporting performance drops. The lower the level of mental anxiety the better the sporting performance is likely to be. You will probably have experienced this for yourself. The less that is whizzing around in your head the easier it is to perform well. The words 'There is too much going on in my head' and 'I have too much on my mind' are frequent reasons for poor performance. The following graph illustrates this point.

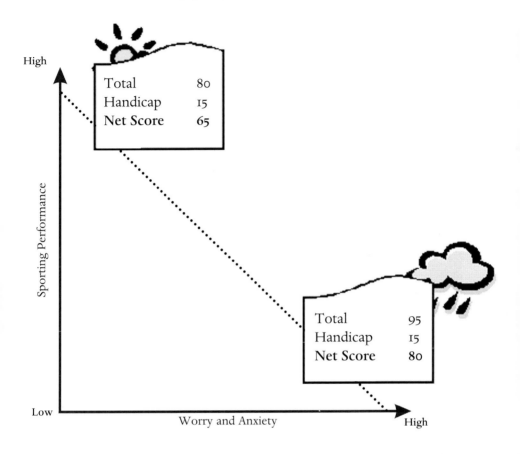

High

Sporting Performance

Total	80
Handicap	15
Net Score	65

Total	95
Handicap	15
Net Score	80

Low

Worry and Anxiety

High

It is clear, therefore, that the real mind threats to playing to the best of our ability are worry, self-doubt and apprehension.

The following thinking skills will help you to keep the right mental attitude before, during and after a golf match. Remember, the attitudes you have are a habit. If these attitudes and thoughts are unrealistic, or overly negative, they will cause you problems. Don't be discouraged, though – they can be changed! You can learn skills to change your attitudes.

Always bear in mind, however, that we learn and perform the complex tasks involved in playing golf best when our anxiety and level of activation are low.

Changing your Attitude

The idea that the way a person reacts to an event depends on their 'attitude' to that event is nothing new. In 300 BC Aristotle wrote:

'Furthermore, whenever we hold the belief that something is terrible or fearsome, we at once experience the corresponding emotion, as also with comforting beliefs.'

And a little later in the first century AD the Greek Stoic Epictetus philosophised that:

'Man is disturbed not by things but by the view he takes of them.'

Now, we don't know if the ancient Greeks would have made good golfers but we can learn from their thinking skills. What Epictetus was implying, and what we now know to be true, is that you can take control of the way you feel and react by learning to develop a more effective attitude towards events. Remember, the attitudes you take in particular situations are a habit and not necessarily consistent with the way things actually are. For example, if you have any easy two-foot putt to win the game, and you take the attitude, *'This is such an easy putt – Anyone could hole it – It would be embarrassing to miss it and be totally humiliated in front of everyone'*. Then, you will feel under pressure and probably will become anxious. You start to worry more and more about how dreadful it will be when you miss this easy putt. As you become more anxious, you feel more stressed and tense – so tense, in fact, that your thought becomes a self-fulfilling prophecy and you will more than likely miss the putt! Very many golfers take this sort of attitude when faced with a pressure situation. But remember, this attitude is just a habit and not necessarily correct. So, if you are prone to this approach get into the opposite habit of questioning and changing this unhelpful attitude. In this case, how do you know you are going to miss the putt? You have certainly sunk many longer and more difficult putts. Since holding this attitude does not help, it's obviously worthwhile trying to change it.

Here are some useful questions to ask yourself if you think you may have some unhelpful attitudes:

> ◻   *Does holding this attitude help my game?*
>
> ◻   *What are the advantages and disadvantages of holding this attitude?*
>
> ◻   *Is there evidence to show that this attitude is incorrect or unrealistic?*
>
> ◻   *Am I jumping to unnecessarily negative conclusions?*
>
> ◻   *Am I concentrating on my weaknesses and neglecting my strengths?*
>
> ◻   *Am I fretting about how things should be instead of accepting them and dealing with them as they are?*
>
> ◻   *Am I predicting the outcome instead of experimenting with it?*

The next step is to develop and use a more realistic and helpful attitude. In the example above, the old attitude could be replaced with: '*OK, here comes a nice easy 2-foot putt – I have sunk loads of these before – this one should roll in nicely if I stay relaxed.*'

If you have the tendency to take overly negative and unhelpful attitudes, then question them, develop a new helpful attitude, then learn it and repeat it frequently until it becomes your natural way of thinking in those situations.

Developing Imagery Skills

When properly used imagery is one of the most powerful mental tools available to a sportsman, and that most certainly includes golfers. Numerous studies have shown that imagery is one of the most effective mental skills for enhancing performance.

As humans, we appear to be able to think in two main ways: that is, sometimes we think in words, and at other times we appear to see pictures or images, in our 'mind's eye'. Imagery simply involves using mental images for a particular purpose. Since we know that negative mental images can have a powerful detrimental effect on us and the way we perform, then it is clear that the ability to control the images we have in our minds should prove a very useful tool. The degree to which any of us think in images varies. Nonetheless, the ability to generate images and use them to practise specific skills can be learned and developed.

Imagery as mental practice

If you haven't the time to get to the practice ground, then mental practice using imagery can be an excellent substitute. Mental practice associated with imagery techniques may be separated into two main types, 'internal' or 'kinaesthetic' imagery, and 'external' or 'visual' imagery. Internal imagery is when you actually imagine yourself carrying out the task from within your own body. You imagine that you can 'feel' yourself performing the task. Indeed, we know that when internal imagery is used effectively, subliminal electrical impulses are sent to the muscles and limbs associated with executing the task. External imagery, on the other hand, is rather like watching a video in which you are one of the players. That is to say you can see yourself hitting a shot in any way, in any setting and under any conditions. You are a spectator watching yourself play.

Learning and using both these techniques can be useful for any golfer. However, internal imagery is found to be most useful for skilled sportsmen. It is likely therefore that the lower your handicap, the more effective you will find this kind of imagery. This is simply because the more skilled a player you are the more likely you are to know what a good swing or correct striking of the ball 'feels' like and looks like. Nonetheless, it is worth all golfers experimenting with both techniques to see which gives the best results.

An imagery exercise

As with most mental skills, it is generally better to learn and practise them initially away from the golf course. When practising and using imagery, you should always endeavour to keep a positive and optimistic attitude. The ability to relax is also an important factor in the effective use of imagery.

The following six step exercise is designed to help you improve your skill to generate and use imagery.

1. Find a quiet and comfortable place where you are unlikely to be disturbed. Seat yourself in a comfortable upright chair. Use your relaxation technique to relax completely. Keep your eyes closed.

2. Practise imagery by first of all visualising a large white surface like a white wall. Visualise the letter 'A' on the surface, then the letter 'B' next to it. Carry on through the alphabet. Observe if any of the letters fade or disappear. If so try and make them stronger.

3. Next practise creating the image of a glass tumbler, fill it with blue liquid, tip out the blue liquid and refill the glass with red liquid, try this with several different colours. Then repeat this but adding ice cubes of a different colour each time.

These first three steps will get you 'warmed up' for the final parts of the exercise.

4. Now imagine a beautiful golf course on a fine sunny day. It may be a course you already know, or one that is completely fictitious, perhaps made up of bits of other golf courses that you have played and enjoyed. Try to picture as much detail as you can, see the trees and lakes, the shape of the fairways, even try to see individual blades of grass. Imagine you can feel the heat of the sun and the breeze on your arms and face. Visualise other golfers on the course. Try to see them in as much detail as possible.

5. Now visualise yourself actually playing on the course. See yourself playing several holes. See yourself playing to the best of your ability and getting a sense of pleasure and achievement from playing. Feel yourself playing, swinging and hitting good shots. Perhaps recreate a past successful round when you played well. Relax and enjoy a feeling of success.

6. Slowly allow the images to fade, take a few deep breaths. Open your eyes and adjust to the outside world.

Vary steps 4 and 5 of this exercise to develop imagery for the following three projects; simulating difficult conditions, coping imagery and positive imagery.

Simulating difficult conditions using imagery

Most golfers would agree that hitting shots on the course is much more difficult than hitting balls on the range. There is no pressure on the practice ground, whereas in actual competitive play each shot 'counts' and you are only allowed one attempt. Plus, there is plenty of time to think about all the things that could go wrong! It will therefore be helpful during a practice session to attempt to recreate some of the pressures that you would experience in a competitive situation, and practise coping with them successfully. Imagery is ideal for this purpose.

Remember you can be the writer and director of your own mental video. You can create an image of the situations you fear or find difficult to handle. Perhaps, for example, you dread that very first tee-shot right in front of the clubhouse. You always feel anxious and invariably your worst nightmare comes true, almost without fail you duff that first drive. A good way to overcome this anxiety would be to take hundreds of drives from this very position. Clearly this is not a practical option, as the greenkeeper will quickly tell you!

However, using vivid imagery you can attempt to recreate this situation on the practice range. So, before starting your practice session, try and visualise yourself standing on the first tee. Imagine that you can see groups of people in and around the clubhouse all watching you. Try to paint this picture in your mind's eye as vividly as possible. As you do so you will feel yourself getting 'keyed up'. Now use your relaxation 'trigger' to reduce the tension and hit some drives. At regular intervals bring your feared image clearly into your mind and then employ your relaxation technique. As you start to hit some reasonable drives you will begin to feel more relaxed and confident about playing from the first tee. This may be the nearest you can get to actual practice on the first tee but you will now have developed a routine which you can use when you get there!

Coping imagery

Elite sportsmen often use a form of imagery where they see themselves performing a task flawlessly. We believe that this strategy, whilst it may work for the professional, could be counterproductive for a handicap player. Instead, we suggest trying a strategy known as coping imagery. The reality is the average club player is going to spend a reasonable proportion of each game in the rough or in bunkers! We suggest that you practise developing imagery where you see yourself successfully coping with these difficulties.

So, if for example, there is a deep bunker on the eighteenth hole which you dread and regularly end up in, develop a visualisation where you see yourself playing a really good recovery shot out of it. This can have the effect of making the bunker appear less of a threat by making you more relaxed as you tee up on that particular hole. Being more relaxed about the playing of the hole should therefore make it less likely that you end up in the bunker in the first place – and if by chance you did, you will have a good mental picture of how easy it is to recover! Which again, hopefully, should help you feel more relaxed....

Positive imagery

This might better be described as optimistic imagery. Positive imagery usually involves visualising a positive or optimistic outcome to a task you are performing. For a professional golfer the visualisations used might be seeing himself or herself performing perfectly, such as scoring birdies at every hole or perhaps winning a major championship. However, you will find that this kind of imagery will probably work best for you if your visualisation is on the 'optimistic side of a *realistic* outcome'. For instance, if you are a high-handicapper playing a 300-yard hole, then visualising driving the green and holing the putt is unlikely to be very helpful as it is something you might achieve once in a million rounds! Try instead to pick an area on the fairway where your ball would realistically land if you hit a good drive. Then, before you actually play the shot, visualise yourself striking the ball and it landing in or just beyond that area. Using imagery in this way you can help yourself to feel more optimistic and relaxed, without setting yourself up for endless failures.

Negative thinking

It is well proven that negative thoughts and attitudes have a detrimental effect on sporting performance. Throughout any game of golf, you should work hard to avoid any negativity. By that we mean you should avoid negative thoughts or being critical about anything, whether it is about yourself, your shots, your partner, the course, the weather or anything else you could possibly think of. At first sight this idea may appear quite extreme and unreasonable, if not downright impossible! Nonetheless, negativity is such a pervasive and destructive force within the human mind it is best left in your locker and banned from the fairways totally!

Well, that is what you have to do, but maybe you knew that already? There is a pretty good chance that you have read or heard about not thinking negatively but did not know how to do it. So, here are some techniques to help you defeat those negative thoughts:

Replace negative thoughts with positive thoughts

Since negative thoughts have a much more powerful effect on us than positive thoughts, we must try to keep negative thoughts out of our minds. This can, however, be quite difficult, as you will know if you have ever tried to put a thought or worry out of your head. As fast as you try to push it out of your mind it tends to pop right back in again! For most of us, the more we try and suppress that worry, the more frustrated and upset we become, and the harder it gets to put that worry out of our mind. So, what is the answer? The answer is to replace that negative thought with a more realistic and positive thought. This is the theory behind 'The Power of Positive Thinking' which is something you may also have heard and read about.

At this point let us give you a gentle warning. Yes, negative and defeatist thinking is associated with a lowered sporting performance. Yes, a more positive and optimistic attitude is generally associated with improved sporting performance. Now here is the big 'but': very strong positive thinking (sometimes called 'mastery') can work well for highly skilled sportsmen, including top golfers, **but** could be unhelpful, if not detrimental, to less skilled handicap golfers.

For example, professional golfers, at the beginning of a round, may hold thoughts in their mind about making perfect shots, breaking the course record or shooting lots of birdies. But, if the average player tried to use these kinds of positive thoughts, it could be counterproductive. First, to an average player, these thoughts would be so unrealistic that they would be difficult to hold in the mind and may subsequently generate a train of negative thoughts. Secondly, again because the thoughts are so unrealistic, the player could be setting himself or herself up for failure, time after time. For most of us, when we consistently fail to achieve or even get close to a goal, we become demoralised.

The solution is to have realistic positive thoughts when the negative thoughts start to crowd in. Try to look for the 'positives' – they will almost always be there! Let us give you two examples of just what we mean.

You put your approach shot into a bunker at the side of the green...

Your usual unhelpful negative thinking might be – 'Oh no! Not in the sand, I am hopeless in bunkers, it will probably take me three or four hacks just to get out of here. Disaster! That's the end of my medal round...' If you hold this thought you are likely to become frustrated, upset and tense and play the shot badly.

A more realistic, positive and helpful thought might be – 'Thank goodness I did some practising with my sand wedge. What a great opportunity to see whether or not I have improved.' or 'Remember that great bunker shot I played last weekend. If I stay relaxed this should come out easily. I can learn from this...'

You are playing an important match and the course is busier than usual with spectators as well as other players.

Your usual unhelpful negative thoughts might be – 'How can I possibly play with all these distractions?' or 'I never play well when people are watching me.'

A more realistic, positive and helpful way of thinking might be – 'Good, there are going to be loads of distractions on the course today, my opponent is probably going to find that difficult. This is a great chance for me to try out the new imagery and relaxation techniques I have learned. This may well give me an advantage.'

Stopping negative thoughts

Because negative thoughts are so powerful, you may sometimes be overwhelmed by negativity and worries and unable to bring in your more realistic and positive thoughts. It is, therefore, vital that you do everything you can to stop this happening. Remember, there is a lot of time during a game of golf for negativity to take hold. Here are some tips to help you:

 Get used to becoming aware when you are being negative or worrying during a game of golf. Develop your own early-warning system, because the sooner you spot this happening, the sooner you can take action!

Develop a mental device to stop the flow of negative thoughts. Imagery is very useful for this purpose. For example, you could develop a mental image of a large neon sign saying STOP. Or perhaps a huge comical greenkeeper holding his hand up and yelling, 'Stop'. As with all imagery, this must be practised first in a quiet place and made as vivid as possible. Bringing a well-rehearsed image like this into your mind will stem the flow of worry.

 Try wearing a rubber band on your wrist, which you could 'ping' when you become aware of negative thoughts running away with you. This can help to re-focus your attention.

 As soon as you have stopped the train of negative thoughts, you **must** quickly replace them with positive thoughts. Maybe use a positive self-statement, (discussed in the section below, 'Positive Self-Talk') followed by some helpful thoughts about the next shot.

Positive Self-Talk

In many ways a number of the earlier techniques we have covered, such as changing negative thoughts for more realistic and positive thoughts, are about 'self-talk'. That is, they are to do with either the running commentary about things that seems to go on in the back of our minds, or the conversations we have with ourselves in our heads. However, in this section we take 'positive self-talk' to refer to special words or phrases which you learn and then repeat back to yourself to achieve a specific result. We will discuss later how positive self-talk can be an important part of focusing attention, but for the moment we will consider three different types of self-talk which are helpful in keeping your mind on the right track:

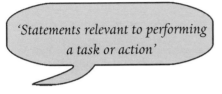

'Statements relevant to performing a task or action' These are statements that you will most likely develop and learn during practice sessions. They will help you to focus attention and perform a particular action in the right way. For example, you might develop a checklist to run through before each shot. This could be along the lines of 'Check distance – Choose club – Decide on target' and could be done in conjunction with a pre-shot routine covering 'Grip – Alignment – Stance etc.'

Take the situation where you have driven off and, as you walk down the fairway, your partner engages you in an earnest discussion about the national economy! You reach your ball and now you must switch your attention to the task of playing the next shot. To help you do this, simply run through your checklist. Then repeat each point again as you perform the tasks. By repeating in your mind the tasks you are doing, you can help guard against being distracted.

'Focusing your Thoughts' on page 45 expands on how this form of positive self-talk can be used to focus attention with examples of the types of checklists that might be used.

'Statements which use mood words containing emotional meaning' Use these statements to help prevent you getting keyed up and tense. On the golf course they will be connected with controlling such feelings as anger, frustration or possibly even over-excitement. Those of you who react badly to setbacks should particularly practise these kinds of statements. For example, you top your drive into the rough in front of the tee. To ward off the flood of negative thoughts and anger at your-

self try and run through your mind some positive self-talk along the lines of: *'Calm, calm, that's no problem, I can fix that, that will be a challenge, it would be great to make a par off that drive, I will stay calm.'*

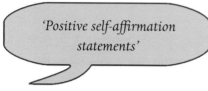

'Positive self-affirmation statements'

These are statements which will help you to feel good about yourself, what you are doing, and how you are doing it. Positive self-affirmation statements are useful to repeat to yourself when nothing else is occupying your mind, and there is the risk of negative thoughts creeping in to fill the vacuum. Obviously there are plenty of moments like this during a round of golf! Examples of such statements which you could develop might be: *'Feeling good – will learn something today – enjoying the challenge – looking forward to using my new relaxation technique.'*

It is sometimes difficult to remember your self-statements, particularly when you first develop them or when under pressure. Don't be afraid to **write** little notes or reminders to yourself that you can keep in your pocket with your score card, or in your golf bag where you will come across them.

Ban self criticism

Ban self criticism totally from your golf. In particular, do not criticise yourself or your performance during a round. Critical analysis of your shots must be confined to the practice ground, where you may be critical of the shot but NEVER of YOURSELF! When we suggest this to some golfers, they are incredulous. They firmly believe that being critical of their performance, getting angry with themselves or 'giving myself a good talking to', helps to correct their mistakes and spur them on to better performance. They may be correct, but somehow we doubt that. Being self-critical tends to raise our emotional level and hence cause tension in our muscles; it makes us more sensitive and easily distracted; it can make us attempt to take more conscious control of the golf swing, resulting in complaints like: 'I'm trying too hard' or 'I'm thinking too much about it.'

You may care to consider this for yourself. If you tend towards being self-critical, which is a habit, you may notice that when you duff a shot and give yourself a hard time about it, you may not play well for the next few shots. If this is the case, you might agree that perhaps self-criticism does not work very well for you. In which case try something different!

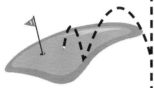

When you hit a bad shot:

- ¤ Refrain from verbally or mentally criticising the stroke or yourself.
- ¤ Refrain, as best you can, from displaying any physical or verbal signs of anger or frustration. This only serves to rehearse and validate the negative feeling and so make it stronger and more detrimental to your performance.
- ¤ Do not comment on or talk about the shot to your partner or your caddie.
- ¤ Immediately try and clear your mind of what has just happened.
- ¤ Be aware of how keyed up you are getting. If you are starting to feel tense, shake yourself out, and reduce tension by using your relaxation technique.
- ¤ Work hard to replace any negative thoughts with realistic and more positive thoughts.

Mind skills on the practice range

The practice ground is the only place where you should be critical of your performance or technique. Nonetheless, even here there are rules about negative thinking and attitude.

In your mind, divide your practice session into two parts. In the first three quarters, say, of the time you have allowed for practice, pay close and critical attention to your skills and techniques. Be aware that, generally, during this type of exercise, you will feel your level of physical activation and tension rising. When this happens and at the end of the session, take a short break. Use your relaxation techniques, focus on a positive and relaxing image and reduce the tension in your muscles. Just walking away from your practice position for a short while may also help you to relax.

Start the final quarter of your practice session with a positive and relaxed attitude, focus on the ball and the target and refrain from technical awareness and criticism. As soon as you have hit several satisfactory shots, finish the session – even if you have some balls left! By finishing with a positive and confident attitude, you are more likely to carry this with you onto the course.

Preparing for that big match

Worry, apprehension, and negative thoughts usually start long before a game begins (this could be days, weeks or even months). This worry generally tends to escalate, as the game gets nearer. By the time you reach the first tee you could be so keyed up and anxious that it is highly unlikely you will play to the best of your ability. As soon as you notice apprehension about a game rising, whether it is hours or even days before the event, you should work hard to curb it using the following techniques:

◻ Check your attitude to the coming game. Is it unrealistic? Is it overly negative? If so, develop a more realistic and positive attitude and practise using it

◻ Make sure you have developed a 'performance goal' for the game (see 'Goal Setting' on page 39) and focus on how you are going to achieve that goal

◻ If you have a worry about a particular hole or hazard, make sure you have developed 'coping imagery' to deal with the problem

◻ If you feel keyed up and tense just before tee off, don't forget to use your relaxation technique.

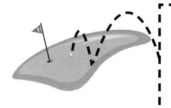

Learn to be aware of your worries and anxieties about a forthcoming golf match and work hard using the techniques you have learned to reduce them.
Controlling your mental anxieties about a game, as soon as they arise, will help to ensure that you are in the best possible mental condition at the beginning of the game.

A word about worry!

Quite a lot of people worry. Quite a lot of people worry a lot! If you are one of these people, it may be helpful to realise that worrying is just a bad habit that you picked up by experience or learned from someone else. If you think back, maybe you can recall that one of your parents was a worrier? What is more, if you are one of these people, you probably find that you worry about most things – not just your golf! Worrying is often used as a problem-solving process and many worriers have very strong beliefs about worry. For example, many people believe that: *'I wouldn't be human if I didn't worry! – Worrying helps me prepare – I must worry about the next match, as it shows that I take my golf seriously and will be ready for any situation that arises.'*

It is beyond the scope of this book to go into the 'whys and wherefores', but we know that worrying is a pointless process. By all means, take your golf seriously, but worrying about it is a poor way to prepare. It may just have the adverse effect of raising your level of tension and apprehension.

3 GOAL SETTING

When researching this book we were frequently asked, 'What's wrong with setting a goal like "Playing under my handicap today" or "Winning this match." What other goals could there be?' Whilst the desire to win can be important, you will see, later in this section, that it is not recommended as the **only** goal to have if you wish to improve your game. We will show that other types of goal setting can be extremely useful in keeping you motivated and encouraged. Indeed, setting the right kinds of goals can help to keep you focused and not too keyed up and anxious during a game. They can also inspire and motivate you during practice.

A good example of the value of goal setting is that of Roger Bannister breaking the four-minute mile. Before this time, the majority of athletes believed that it was not possible to run a mile in under four minutes, so no one did! Bannister believed otherwise and set the goal of proving it by studying and changing his running technique.

History records that Bannister achieved his goal in May 1954. Interestingly enough, in the months that followed, a number of other top athletes around the world also ran a mile in under four minutes but without changing their running style. The only thing that changed was that they believed it was an achievable goal.

The main ways in which goal setting can help your performance are by:

◻ **Directing attention** – goal setting can help you to focus attention upon the selected task and upon achieving the goal relative to that task

◻ **Focusing effort** – if you have set yourself a reasonably difficult goal, then you are going to have to work at achieving it

◻ **Increasing patience and persistence** – as rewards will not be immediate, goal setting can help create the drive to sustain effort for longer periods

◻ **Promoting the learning of new skills** – to achieve a difficult goal often requires new learning skills, techniques and knowledge.

Whatever you want out of your golf, whether it is reducing your handicap or just having more relaxation and enjoyment, it will best be achieved by setting appropriate goals. However, to be effective, goal setting must be done in a specific and organised manner and defined in terms of very clear characteristics.

So, let us say you wish to become a better player and set the goal to 'become a better player'. On the face of it, this seems to be a worthwhile goal. However, a number of characteristics about it make it difficult to achieve. The goal is very general, impossible to measure and unclear as to how and when the goal is to be obtained. So, how could setting this goal be improved? Since becoming a better player involves improving several physical and mental skills, it is necessary to set several specific goals, each defined in measurable terms.

For example, a skills analysis might reveal that the weakest part of your game is your tee-shot. So, this might be a good place to start with your goal setting. If you are currently only hitting two or three fairways each round, your new improved goal could, at the start of the year, be *'To get three out of four of my tee-shots on the fairway by next September.'* This is a better goal because it is specific, measurable and attainable.

All that is left is to define some short-term goals that will help you on the way to achieving that final goal. Your intermediate goal could therefore be *'To get one in every two tee shots in play by April'*. To keep track, you could take a scorecard with you every round and award yourself a tick against each hole where you hit the fairway.

The basic principles of goal setting

There are a number of vital things to be considered when goal setting. The following basic principles have been gleaned from research conducted in industrial, organisational, academic, sport and exercise settings:

◻ *It is important that the goal is set and accepted by you*
That is, it is not one forced upon you by someone else. It is important to believe that the goal is yours and is something you genuinely wish to achieve. Spend some time thinking about setting useful goals. For example, look at the weaknesses in your game. What goals would address these? Write the goals down.

◻ *Specific goals are better than general goals*
If it is too difficult to see whether or not progress has been made, then that goal has not been made specific. You are therefore likely to become discouraged and fail to improve.

◻ *Goals should be measurable*
As well as being specific, goals should be measurable. How can you truly know if a goal has been achieved if it cannot be measured? So try and define your goals in terms of numbers, distances, percentages etc. For example, percentage of fairways hit, number of iron shots on target, percentage of short putts holed, etc.

◻ *Moderately difficult to difficult goals are better than easy goals*
A vast body of research points to the importance of challenging sportsmen to strive for goals that appear to be difficult to achieve. So, in setting your goals to improve your golf try and set goals for which you have to struggle. Having said that, do not constantly set goals, which are so difficult that no matter how hard you strive to achieve them you regularly fail. If you do this you will rapidly become disheartened.

◻ *Set 'performance' goals rather than 'outcome goals'*
Research has consistently supported the setting of 'performance' goals, as opposed to having only 'outcome' goals. Performance goals refer to methods and strategies designed to help achieve skill mastery. These are goals that can be achieved even if you don't win the event. Golfers who have a performance goal orientation tend to think in terms of quality of performance, and not necessarily just in terms of the outcome of the competition, i.e. winning or losing. Even top professionals who have a very strong desire to win can often be heard saying in an interview something like, 'I know I got beaten today but I was beginning to feel more comfortable with my new swing, and I hit more greens in regulation than average.'

The desire to win is healthy, but if winning is your only goal for a match the pressure of this, particularly if you are behind at some point during the game, could lead to over anxiety and de-motivation. It is easier to avoid becoming negative and discouraged if you are achieving performance goals.

LOSE BUT STILL WIN!

Let's say you are in a match and you have set a personal performance goal of getting over 50% of your tee shots on the fairway. You can still achieve this goal even if you lose the match you are playing. So, whilst you will be somewhat disappointed at losing there is considerable consolation in achieving your personal goal.

We strongly advise that in all rounds of golf you play, you set a personal performance oriented goal. This will mean that, even if you do lose the match, you will have improved your skills or at least learned where you have difficulties. By setting this type of goal you are more likely to improve your skills, obtain a sense of achievement from your game and as a bonus, improve your chances of winning!

◻ *Use short-term goals to achieve long-term goals*

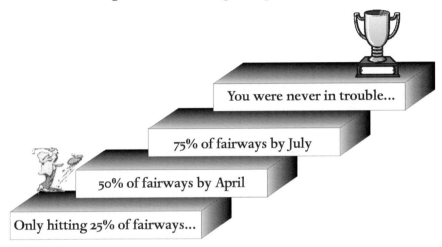

Staying motivated for long-term goals can sometimes be difficult. By setting and achieving intermediate short-term goals you are more likely to feel motivated to hang in for the long haul and achieve ultimate success.

◻ *Mechanism for achieving goals*

It is vital that, having set a goal, a specific strategy or plan is developed for achieving that goal. So, how do you set about achieving the above goal of hitting more fairways? If left to chance, it will most likely never happen. You must work to devise a plan for achieving this goal, possibly with the help of the club professional or a more experienced player. Your plan might include such things as:

• Using an iron or a 5 wood off some tees

• Teeing up on the left side of the teeing ground if you tend to hook the ball and vice versa

- Taking lessons from your professional to improve your technique

Whatever elements are in your plan we strongly recommend that you write down your specific goal, your short-term goals, and how you will measure and record progress. Regularly monitor how things are going, and seek more advice/help if necessary. As you see improvements coming through these will help provide you with additional motivation to achieve your specific goal.

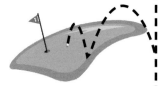

You will achieve more and get more from your golf if you set yourself specific goals that are not related to your score or the result of a match. Only having outcome goals such as 'winning the match' or 'lowering my handicap' will normally increase pressure and tension and so reduce your performance.

Set yourself realistic goals that are related to improving your skills. You will find the results will improve more quickly if you leave them to take care of themselves!

4   FOCUSING YOUR THOUGHTS

The single most important mental skill for sporting success is, most probably, the ability to concentrate on, or pay close attention to, the task in hand whilst being able to ignore all other distractions. This skill is often called 'selective attention'. As with other skills, it can be learned, practised and improved. The ability to direct this attention and to either broaden or narrow it as required is called 'attentional focus'.

Attentional focus can be directed externally, that is out towards the surrounding environment, or internally, which is paying attention to what is going on in your mind and body. Sportsmen who appear to be concentrating very hard on a task are often described as being 'focused'. Golfers who master these focusing skills will tend to play to the best of their ability more frequently.

In many ways you can consider your attention (or concentration) as being like a pair of binoculars which you can point in any direction and clearly focus on any scene. Learning to direct your attention in this very focused way helps to block out unwanted distractions, especially negative thoughts, and highlights what is required to attain your immediate goal.

Focusing is best achieved by using a 'routine' that ideally starts when you arrive at your ball. Let us, therefore, look at the sequence of actions that we suggest need to be organised into what is known as a 'shot routine'. Imagine you are walking towards your ball in preparation for your second shot to the green:

1. For the past few minutes your attention has been focused on a conversation with your partner. You must now 'switch' your attention to the shot you have to play. In other words 'switch on'. Your focus needs to be directed externally, out into the environment, in a very

broad manner, as you take in varied information about such things as the lie of the ball, the position of bunkers and other hazards, distances, wind direction and so on.

2. You then need to focus your attention internally and use your judgement to decide which club, and type of shot, is most likely to produce the desired result (this obviously depends on your ability and experience).

3. Next, you have to focus inwards again and check to see if you are getting keyed up and whether there are any areas of tension in your body, e.g. increased grip pressure. If you think you may be a little over tense, then take a few moments to adjust this using your relaxation technique.

4. As you come up to the ball you will need a few moments to use your visualisation skills to 'feel' yourself playing the shot and 'see' the ball landing in the target area.

5. Next you go through your usual address procedure (which may include grip, alignment, and stance checks), and hit the ball.

6. You now need to 'switch off' your attention. Whatever the outcome of the shot you should try and repeat some calming and encouraging self-statements and relax your focus.

The six actions above need to be organised into an easily remembered routine. To develop such a 'shot routine', you will need to experiment, design and rehearse techniques that work for you. The best results will be achieved if you work on these away from the course. It might also prove helpful if you adapt your shot routine for different types of shots. We will give you some hints about doing this at the end of this section.

One point that we cannot emphasise enough is that once you have developed a routine you must use it **consistently**. Most human beings – and that includes golfers! – find that changes in routine can make us feel anxious and uncomfortable. Conversely, when things are normal and familiar we feel more at ease. A golf match is full of pressures and uncertainties; by using the same routines you can bring along some of the familiarity and comfort of the practice range.

Here are some techniques to consider when designing your routine:

Centering

Your ability to focus attention or concentrate on a particular shot will be best when your level of physical activation is low, that is, when your body is relaxed and free from tension. So, when you are preparing to play a shot, check your body for tension and relax it if necessary using your relaxation trigger. Also, learn to focus attention on your own thoughts, learn to be an observer of what kind of thoughts you are having. If they are worries, anxieties or any kind of negative thought whatsoever then use the mind skills described in 'Getting your Thinking Right' (page 20) to stop them and change them for positive thoughts. This will keep your mind and body more relaxed and able to focus on the task in hand. Plus, you will be less easily distracted.

Many top sportsmen use a process sometimes known as 'centering' to achieve the above. Centering involves focusing your attention on an area a few centimetres below your navel, but inside your body, which 'feels' like your centre of gravity. Try and become aware of being able to feel this point. After a few moments your attention will be focused internally and you will be more aware of what is going on in your mind and body.

Switching attention

The ability to 'switch' the focus of your attention quickly, efficiently and totally is a very important skill for a golfer. For example, as you approach your ball for a shot you will need to switch your attention to your 'shot routine'. So, try to make the 'switch' as clearly defined as possible. You may find it useful to develop some kind of mental device which will help you do this.

For instance, when you are ready to switch your attention, you could use a mental image of a large switch or lever being thrown, rather like changing the points on a railway track or a light being turned on. For those of you who prefer to think in a more verbal way you could develop and use specific statements, that will signal a change in attention. For example, you could say clearly and loudly in your mind something like, 'Now it is shot time' or 'Now I am in the shot zone.' The important thing is that you must always use the same 'switching device' to switch your attention.

Resting between shots

Concentration and selective attention require energy and can be mentally tiring. It is totally unnecessary, not to say exhausting, to try and focus constantly throughout a whole round. As the legendary Walter Hagen used to say: 'Take time to smell the flowers.' So, rest your mind between shots. Enjoy the countryside, the flowers, the birds, the sky, etc. This will help you stay positive, have fun, and avoid negativity, safe in the knowledge that, no matter what you have been doing or thinking, you can, when required, re-focus your attention.

And remember to take it 'one shot at a time'.

Mental checklists

It is all very well having the ability to switch your attention, but it is necessary to be absolutely clear, for any particular task, what it is you actually need to pay attention to! It is far easier to concentrate on a task when that task is clearly defined. To help in this process, you could develop a mental checklist of information, not only for your standard shot routine, but also for various specialist shots as well.

Such a checklist would gather the information needed to make an informed decision on the best shot to play, taking into account your capabilities. For example, your ball ends up in the rough. As part of your standard shot routine you might have a 'trouble shot checklist' that reads something like this:

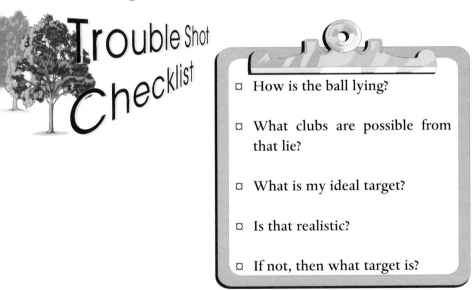

Trouble Shot Checklist

- ☐ How is the ball lying?

- ☐ What clubs are possible from that lie?

- ☐ What is my ideal target?

- ☐ Is that realistic?

- ☐ If not, then what target is?

You may already do these checks. However, by making the list checking a fixed and identifiable task, it is easier to focus and block out any distractions.

Switching attention smoothly

It is important that your attention switches smoothly, yet quickly, from one task to another. This will help you to avoid being distracted, or give space for negative thoughts such as 'self doubt' to creep into your mind. It is advisable to design and practise your shot routine in such a way that you always play the shot immediately at the end of the 'shot routine'. **Do not hesitate and give negativity a way in!**

Re-focusing

A very important skill to develop is something called 're-focusing'. The fact of the matter is, that no matter how good your concentration, there will be times when your routine will be broken, or you will be distracted by external events. For example, it would be very unwise to go ahead with your shot routine if someone started walking across the fairway in front of you! Re-focusing is the skill of waiting for the distraction to end and starting the task again as if nothing had happened.

Distractions can take all forms: a dog running around, people talking loudly, a plane flying over, even an unpleasant smell drifting over the course! Whatever it is, when you have to re-focus, work very hard to avoid any kind of emotional reaction. Getting angry or upset will only have a negative effect on you. Try using your thinking skills, relaxation technique, positive self-statements. Or make a joke of it and laugh it off, try anything, **but do not react negatively**. When the distraction is over, check your tension level and start your routine from the beginning. **You should think and act as if this is a start not a restart.**

If the distraction is likely to continue – for example, the local brass band has decided to march up and down alongside the course – accept the new sounds. Allow them to merge and become part of your playing environment, before starting again.

Practising under pressure

Once you have developed and learned concentration, focusing and centering skills you should practise them under pressure. The more and varied pressures and distractions which you can use during a practice session, the better prepared you will be for using your skills in the heat of competition. You could, for example, build on the pressure you are under during putting practice by having to sink say, ten balls in a row and if you miss one having to start from the beginning. You could also use your imagination to picture yourself in a high pressure situation.

We have all imagined having a short putt to win the Open, but why not try a tricky six footer to win the Medal or the Club Championship? It might prove much harder, because it is more realistic! To help you cope with distractions have someone talk to you or try and distract you whilst you are practising putting or hitting shots on the range. This will help you to practise your routine in extreme conditions.

Importance of a routine

A 'shot routine' is a specific set of tasks that you **always** carry out before commencing your swing. We have repeatedly highlighted how important such a routine is in ensuring your attention is focused. But if you are still in any doubt, think about what you do when you are faced with a vital shot. When you are under pressure, do you give the shot more care than normal? Do you take more time over it? Do you have some extra practice swings? Do you think – *This is crucial. I had better have an extra practice swing – or – I had better get this over with quick?*

Whatever it is you do or think under pressure, if it is different from your usual preparation then it is more than likely you will neither be relaxed nor focused, resulting in a poor shot. Far better to have a consistent routine which means that each shot in a round can be treated equally whether it is the putt to win the match or a simple chip to the first green. This will help to remove the worry or anxiety about what to do when faced with a vital shot. You know what you are going to do...

Simply switch into your routine!

All that we have said about what could be included in a 'shot routine' may lead you to think that using one might make you hold up the whole course! Rest assured it won't. You will find that as you practise and refine your routine, it will become second nature and the whole process will take no longer than your normal shot procedure. It might even make you a faster player as you know what you are going to do!

However you design your routine, make sure it feels natural and comfortable for you. If necessary use checklists and mnemonics like GAS (Grip, Alignment, Stance) as memory aids.

Any routine should be tailor made for you – by you. You don't have to include everything we've talked about! However, we strongly rec-ommend you try and include the following elements in your standard shot routine:

- ❑ 'Switching on' technique
- ❑ A check for tension, use relaxation technique if necessary
- ❑ Focusing on external information relevant to the shot
- ❑ Visualising the shot
- ❑ The chance to practise a swing which will achieve the desired results.

To help you design your own routine we have shown opposite an exam-ple of a standard 'shot routine' and how it can be adapted for other shots such as putting and trouble shots.

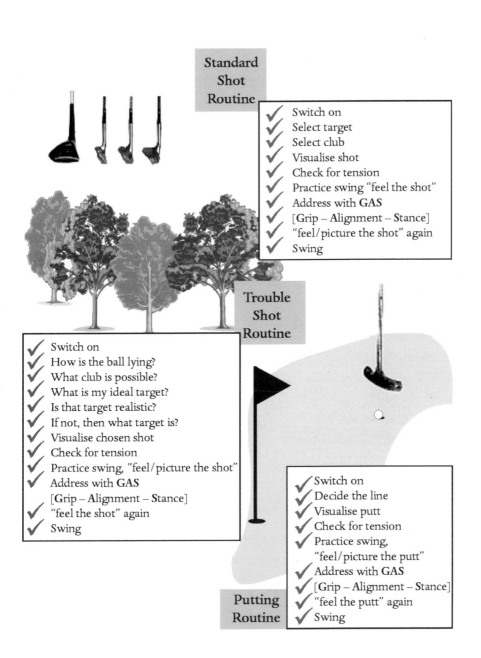

Standard Shot Routine

✓ Switch on
✓ Select target
✓ Select club
✓ Visualise shot
✓ Check for tension
✓ Practice swing "feel the shot"
✓ Address with **GAS**
✓ [Grip – Alignment – Stance]
✓ "feel/picture the shot" again
✓ Swing

Trouble Shot Routine

✓ Switch on
✓ How is the ball lying?
✓ What club is possible?
✓ What is my ideal target?
✓ Is that target realistic?
✓ If not, then what target is?
✓ Visualise chosen shot
✓ Check for tension
✓ Practice swing, "feel/picture the shot"
✓ Address with **GAS**
✓ [Grip – Alignment – Stance]
✓ "feel the shot" again
✓ Swing

Putting Routine

✓ Switch on
✓ Decide the line
✓ Visualise putt
✓ Check for tension
✓ Practice swing, "feel/picture the putt"
✓ Address with **GAS**
✓ [Grip – Alignment – Stance]
✓ "feel the putt" again
✓ Swing

> Focusing your attention on the shot in hand is probably the most important mental skill for golf.
> The best way of achieving this is by developing a 'shot routine' which you apply consistently.

Finally, what should you think about when you are swinging?

When asked this question, the 1920 Open Champion George Duncan famously replied, 'Nothing at all.' Ideally this is what you should do! Just switch onto 'automatic pilot' and let your swing flow naturally and uninhibited. Unfortunately, not all golfers are capable of doing this, as Nature abhors a vacuum and tries to fill that empty space with thoughts about how the swing is to be carried out!

Thinking about 'how to swing' whilst actually swinging is to be avoided at all costs. Don't tell yourself to do things like *Keep your left arm straight, head steady, turn your hips etc.* Sports psychologists call this type of thinking 'volitional control', and point out that in most instances it leads to poor performance. Thinking about how to make the swing movement usually causes a stiff, wooden, jerky swing with no balance or rhythm. Clearing the mind induces a natural free flowing swing with good tempo.

So how best can the vacuum be filled? Well, most golfers have probably already answered that for themselves by devising what are usually referred to as 'swing thoughts'. These are usually thoughts which have been used at times when the golfer was playing well, and he or she believes in them as an instant cure for poor performance. Such 'swing thoughts' can be helpful in avoiding volitional control and if used correctly they can improve consistency in your swing.

A swing thought
is for life...

If you need to employ a 'swing thought' then you should think of something that helps the rhythm and tempo of the swing. For example, you could try counting **one, two** as you make your backswing and a long thre...ee...ee... as you smoothly accelerate down and through the ball. Or perhaps you could hum a tune? Sam Snead was reputed to use The Blue Danube Waltz as his 'swing thought'!

The ultimate aim is to find something that suits you, and stick with it through thick and thin. The benefit of using one 'swing thought' only is that it will become part of your make-up, part of your swing, and part of your skills. The single 'swing thought' will take its rightful place as part of your golf game. It is the part of your skills which prevents volitional control and allows your swing to flow. Believe in your 'swing thought' and you will develop greater consistency, free from searching for a new 'instant cure' swing thought every time your game goes off the boil!

When you feel your swing is out of balance or rhythm simply experiment by fine-tuning the speed of your 'swing thought'. A little faster or a little slower should soon have you back on track.

TAKING RESPONSIBILITY

Put yourself in these two situations. What would your answers be?

A You have played poorly and have lost to someone you should have beaten easily. In the clubhouse everyone is teasing you and asking – *'How could you lose to old Jim? He can't even break 100!'*

B You have just won an important competition and when you are presented with the trophy you are asked – *'To what do you attribute your great play here today?'*

The reasons or excuses you give in response to these kinds of questions are highly significant and indicate the level to which you **believe** you are responsible. As with the patterns of thinking discussed earlier, these reasons, or 'attributions', are a habit and may not necessarily be correct or helpful. The purpose of this section is to show you how to use 'attributions' which lead to a greater expectancy of success and greater effort at your game.

Attributions

In answering the question posed in situation 'A' most people will find it very difficult to admit to their mistakes or failings. If we do something silly or make a mistake, we may worry that others will think we're stupid and that perhaps we really are stupid! – a thought that is very painful and damaging to self confidence. The reality, of course, is that normal people don't suddenly become total idiots simply because they make a mistake or do something silly! Nonetheless, most individuals, and particularly golfers, will come up with reasons and excuses for a poor performance or making a mistake to avoid feeling badly about themselves.

So excuses for losing to old Jim might include, 'My back was giving me trouble...' or 'It was so slow, how could anyone concentrate...' Perhaps by attributing a poor performance to something beyond our control, such as 'slow play' or 'bad luck', we hope it may be better next time. Although this may not be the best solution, we believe it is better than attributing poor performance to something like 'lack of talent' or 'lack of ability', which may be saying that the result will be the same next time. An admission that would be both painful and discouraging!

Well, that is poor performance, but to what do you usually attribute a good performance? How would you respond in scenario 'B'? This may depend, to a large degree, on such factors as your gender, age or what culture you were brought up in. However, it is not uncommon for many of us to be very modest about success. Perhaps we have been told, 'Don't get big headed' or 'Don't get too full of yourself' or that 'Pride comes before a fall...' Therefore, we may play down our success and again attribute it to something transitory like chance by saying, 'I was just very lucky today', or 'My opponent played so badly today it made me look good'.

The kinds of 'attributions' discussed above are often described as 'external', that is success or failure is attributed to something that is outside us or out of our control. Furthermore these attributions are very common, quite understandable and, by seeming to protect our self esteem, may work – **in the short term!**

To build something for the long term it is important to realise that:

If you do not accept responsibility for errors and failures and don't credit yourself with success – how can you possibly hope to improve your game?

Researchers monitoring the behaviour of top sportsmen, including professional golfers, have shown that:

'You are more likely to improve all aspects of your game, especially consistency, if you accept responsibility for your actions whether they result in success or failure'

Therefore to improve you should learn to attribute the results to 'internal' factors. In other words, things over which you have control.

Taking control

As with all our other ways of thinking, the attributions we make are habits we have got into and find difficult to break. However these habits can be changed. By following the suggestions below you can learn the effective new skill of **taking responsibility for** and **control of** your game. As with making any changes, it may seem difficult and perhaps feel uncomfortable and unnatural to start with. But, as with all the other mental skills we have discussed, if you persist and practise it will soon feel 'like you'.

There are four simple steps to taking responsibility for and control of your game:

> **I** List the reasons or 'attributions' you usually give now, to your-
> self and other people, when you play well and when you play
> badly. Ask yourself whether these reasons are helpful or not.

◻ *Make notes*
   Pay attention to what you say and write   Some Tips to **Help**
   things down for a few weeks in a note-
   book. When you play badly do you take
   responsibility for your mistakes or do you make excuses? If you have just
   played well and everyone is slapping you on the back, make a note of how
   you respond. Do you discount your achievement?

◻ *Identify UNHELPFUL reasons for:*

(i) <u>*Failure*</u> *– Generally, the kinds of reasons or attributions you might give for*
   failure that are **unhelpful** *would be either:*
   (a) <u>internal and uncontrollable</u> (that is something bad you believe you can't
   change), e.g., 'I'm just no good at this'
   or
   (b) <u>external</u>', e.g. 'He was trying to put me off all the way round.'
   Reasons that are 'internal and uncontrollable' are unhelpful because they
   are de-motivating, and prevent you learning from your mistakes. 'External'
   reasons are similarly unhelpful as they deny responsibility for a poor per-
   formance and hold you back from making the necessary effort to improve
   your game.

(ii) <u>*Success*</u> *– Usually the reasons or attributions you may give for success that*
   are **unhelpful** *would be 'external'. In other words, things that are out of*
   your control, e.g., 'It was just my lucky day' or ' My opponent played very
   poorly.' These reasons are **unhelpful** *because you are implying that the*
   same result may not necessarily happen again or, worse still, that you may
   not remember what you did differently that worked so well!

2 Develop reasons or 'attributions' that might lead you to expect to be able to do better and make more effort next time.

☐ *Think of new reasons*
If you discover that some of your current **Some Tips to Help**
reasons or attributions may be unhelpful,
try and think of some new reasons for
failure and success that, if they were true and you believed them 100%,
would make you feel you could try harder and do better next time.

☐ *Examples of HELPFUL reasons for:*
(i) <u>Failure</u> – *More helpful attributions for failure or poor performance should be 'internal and controllable' (that is bad things that can be changed), e.g. 'Yes, I did not play well today, I lost my cool and did not always use my shot routine. I will make every effort to ensure that next time I stick to my routine all the way round.'*

(ii) <u>Success</u> – *More helpful attributions for success should be 'internal' and personal, e.g. 'Yes, I concentrated hard today and used my new focusing skills well' or 'I prepared thoroughly for this match and brought it all together on the day.'*

3 Start to make the changes in your attributions by convincing yourself the new ones would be better.

You probably believe that the reasons you **Some Tips to Help**
habitually give for success and failure are
true and the best way of looking after
yourself. Giving up these beliefs is difficult. Spend some time thinking about them, debate with yourself. Write down the pros and cons of each one. Maybe even discuss them with someone who uses different attributions. If you are honest with yourself you will soon start to see that giving yourself

credit for your good performances and 'standing up and being counted' for your bad ones is going to be beneficial for your self belief and therefore your golf game.

4   Practise giving the new reasons in all situations until they feel 'like you'.

Some Tips to Help

☐ *Old habits die hard*
When people first try to learn the changes
in thinking that we suggest in this book,
they frequently say, 'Yes I agree. I know in my mind that the new way of thinking could be better but it just doesn't feel right.' So, you may well find that when you first start to make changes in your attributions for good or bad performances that it will feel odd and uncomfortable. That is because you are changing a comfortable old habit – probably a bad habit!

☐ *Practice makes perfect*
Perhaps at some time you have changed a technical aspect of your game. Maybe you changed your grip or swing at the suggestion of the club professional. At first it probably felt awkward and strange but if you recall, the more you practised the more comfortable it felt and, hopefully your game improved. It is just the same with learning new thinking skills. Once you have decided on new attributions you must use them and practise them until they feel comfortable.

☐ *Don't be afraid*
Take every opportunity to practise your new attitude. If you have played poorly, don't shy away from it, don't make excuses, admit to what went wrong and learn from it. It's worth it! Because that is going to help you improve your game! To start with, it may be difficult and you may feel embarrassed about playing badly but once you learn to take responsibility

for the quality of your game you will start to feel more self assured and confident – even in the face of a ribbing in the clubhouse!

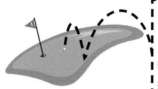

YOUR GAME WILL IMPROVE IF YOU:

- ¤ Take responsibility
- ¤ Give yourself credit for your good performances
- ¤ 'Stand up and be counted' on your bad days
- ¤ Remove any talk of 'superstition' and 'luck'
- ¤ Are honest with yourself.

6 BUILDING CONFIDENCE

Over the years a great deal of research has been done on the mental factors involved in sporting performance, now popularly referred to as sports psychology. Some of these studies have been looking specifically at motivation and self-confidence. One very important point came out of this. Although hardly surprising, the research confirmed that:

'Sportsmen who are self-confident and are expecting to succeed are generally those most likely to succeed'

Interestingly, this principle seems to apply irrespective of the individual's level of skill. So, self-confidence is important whether you are a top professional playing in the Ryder Cup or a junior learning the basics of grip and swing.

In some ways this section on confidence building brings together many of the ideas and skills discussed in the earlier sections of this chapter. It is aimed at reminding you to always be conscious of trying to build your own confidence. You will find that, as you learn and apply the mental skills in this book, you can begin to master your fears and feel more in control of your game. Consequently, your self-confidence will increase both on and off the golf course. As this happens, you should feel a greater sense of achievement and enjoyment from your game. This, in itself, can motivate you to improve your golf skills and work at improving those areas you may find difficult or daunting. Ultimately, this should help you play closer to your potential more often.

Developing confidence from your thinking skills

You can use the mental skills outlined in the previous sections to ensure that you think about yourself and what you are doing in a positive and constructive way. Many golfers lack self-confidence as a result of negative sporting experiences in the past, probably at school. Many youngsters were made to feel humiliated and inferior if they performed poorly at sporting tasks. These kinds of experiences often stick with us, so that when we play off the first tee in front of a crowd of people, for example, we may feel tense and anxious. Using the skills from the earlier sections, you can overcome this 'conditioning' and rebuild your self-confidence. Remember that a golfer who is self-confident as a result of using these thinking skills to deal with negative thoughts will believe that they are **not only competent to play the shot to the best of their current ability, but are also not overly concerned should they strike the ball badly**. He or she will, of course, also be employing techniques which make them more relaxed and focused, and thus more likely to play the shot well!

Using success to build confidence

Self-confidence is also increased by successful performance. As the saying goes: 'Nothing breeds success like success'. But, here again, you can use the skills in this book to ensure you experience more success and thus build confidence. On this point it is important to bear in mind that success is relative and, depending on how you define success, you can set yourself up to succeed or fail. If you define succeeding as 'Hitting a drive like

Tiger Woods' then you will probably always fail and become demoralised and de-motivated. But, by redefining success, i.e. using performance goals (as previously described in 'Goal Setting'), you have the opportunity to experience success as often as possible and therefore build confidence. Do not set goals that are clearly unattainable!

How to build confidence

There are many strategies that you can use to build your self-confidence and motivation. By learning and applying the mental skills from the previous sections your confidence will grow, but to help you, here are some techniques specifically designed for building confidence in your golf game:

◻ Set goals for practice sessions so that you can experience success as often as possible.

◻ Redefine 'success' in a competitive round to **include** positive outcomes other than simply winning. For example: 'Another chance to develop my mental skills', 'More experience in using my shot routines', 'An opportunity to meet a challenge and have fun'. The latter is usually a forgotten goal!

◻ Try and finish a practice session after you have hit several good shots, even if it means finishing earlier than you intended! Come away feeling confident and that the session has been a success.

◻ Sometimes we reinforce our lack of confidence by acting in an unsure and hesitant manner. To counteract this, try acting 'as – if' confident. This technique might sound strange, but can be very effective for some people. Study golfers that you think look confident, note what they do and don't do. What is it that makes them **look** confident? Now imagine that you are self-confident. What would you look like? How would you behave? What mannerisms would you exhibit? When you have gathered this information, use it to act 'as-if' you are confident. You might be surprised how effective this technique can be. Furthermore, it may give you a winning edge by unsettling your opponent!

◻ Sit down and think of the reasons why you play golf. Are you really getting out of it what you want? If not, why not? Perhaps you need to rethink your goals? This exercise can often help to revitalise flagging motivation.

◻ If you are easily embarrassed and fear playing bad shots, confront that fear, because it can become a self-fulfilling prophecy! If you play poorly or hit a terrible shot, point it out, be open about it. Make sure you hold in your mind the idea that it was 'just a bad shot' and does not reflect on you personally beyond that. Playing a bad shot or having a bad round doesn't affect your standing as a person or a golfer. As we all know, even the best players in the world can hit horrendous shots and have nightmare rounds!

◻ Try going out and deliberately playing badly for several games. It will give you a chance to convince yourself that you can survive such happenings without your world falling apart! If you do this on your own it will also help you cope with letting other golfers play through!

◻ Do not be overly critical about yourself. Make all criticism constructive, encouraging and supportive. Talk to yourself as you would wish a good motivating coach or caddy to talk to you.

◻ If there are certain types of shots you fear, then make sure you practise them. If you are afraid of bunkers, for example, you could organise a lesson on bunker play from your professional, and then play a round of golf trying to put yourself in as many bunkers as possible. Once you start to play more good bunker shots you will build confidence, your fear of bunkers should be reduced, and therefore you will probably be less likely to end up in them in the first place!

◻ Identify the holes that cause you trouble and prepare a sensible strategy for playing them. This will stop you worrying about them in advance. You will be more confident about playing these potential 'disaster holes' as you have a plan to carry you through.

◻ When deciding which shot to play during your pre-shot routine, choose a shot which you feel confident of executing. Don't attempt a shot that you have doubts about. Thinking *'It might come off...'* will lead to negativity and most probably a poor result. For example, instead of 'going for the green', consider adopting a more sensible strategy which you know you can achieve, like laying up short of potential trouble, and hopefully geting down with a chip and a putt. When you complete the hole safely you will have experienced success, and your self-confidence will be growing...

FINALLY...

We want to remind you of three things. Firstly, none of the mental skills we have suggested will be of any use whatsoever in improving your golf **unless you use them and practise them!** Secondly, that when you begin using some of the techniques we have outlined they may feel strange and uncomfortable. Don't give up! Just like a new pair of shoes it won't be long before you get used to them and they become an accepted part of your golfing armoury. We are confident that for a little bit of effort you will experience a big improvement in your ability to meet and beat golf's mental hazards. And lastly...

> **Always remember that human beings are highly motivated by pleasure. So make sure you are enjoying your golf, that way you will keep your motivation to improve on the up!**

THE DIZZY HEIGHTS CASEBOOK

– I was going well, then –
– This needs 101% –
– Derek's better on his own! –
– Disaster is always round the corner –
– When the red mist comes doon... –
– I knew I was going to do that... –
– Steve doesn't 'give it a go' any longer –
– I always feel I'm rushing... –
– Janie has a thing about bunkers –
– Wise after the event –
– What's that sound? –
– The 'bogey hole' –
– Is there a god of golf? –
– Bob's dream turns into a nightmare! –
– The last minute dash! –
– John's putting touch disappears! –
– How can I play with all this noise? –
– I don't deserve to win... –
– Who's going to come second? –
– I might never live this down –

DIZZY HEIGHTS GOLF CLUB
Bunker Hill
Topping
Barks.

Dear Readers,

When we allowed the researchers of Golf Between the Ears to visit our club they assured us they would protect the identity of our members when the book went into print. I would ask you to respect this wish and treat anything you read in this section as private and confidential. Not everyone here at Dizzy Heights is mad!

Yours faithfully,

Horatio Mindblower

Rear Admiral Horatio Mindblower
President, Dizzy Heights Golf Club

THE DIZZY HEIGHTS CASEBOOK

Welcome to the Dizzy Heights Casebook. To create this collection of personal experiences we went out and talked to golfers of all ages and abilities. They told us about deep-seated fears, mental blocks, the things that upset them. In short, they told us of all the mental problems that were ruining their enjoyment of the game. Look and see if you recognise any of the difficulties they have encountered. Maybe you or someone in your Sunday morning fourball has experienced the same thing? If so, help is at hand! Each of the problems is discussed and a solution suggested with references to the relevant sections of The Basic Mental Skills. So, read on. Perhaps the answer you have been looking for is just a couple of pages away!

I WAS GOING WELL, THEN...

It was Medal Finals Day and Alec was relating to Barry, the young assistant professional, how he had played.

'I was going really well – four inside my handicap at the turn. Then suddenly, I thought, I don't want to mess up this good score. My mind told me to start playing cautiously – hold on to what you've got! I somehow changed my approach to the shots – *Don't go over there in the trees I might lose a ball...Just play to the left where the rough's not too thick.* I seemed to go on the defensive, afraid of ruining the good score I appeared to be heading for... *but that's what happened!!* Instead of continuing to play in the relaxed manner which had me scoring well, I changed to a tense "try not to make any mistakes" attitude which put me under pressure, and I went completely to pieces. I finished way over my handicap.'

'The mind's always playing tricks,' observed Barry. 'Mine especially,' sighed Alec. 'This has happened before, you know. I start to think about how well things are going and I just want to finish there and then so that everyone can see my good scoring. If only I could keep playing the same way and not become over defensive, which seems to lead to disaster.'

Explaining Alec's collapse

When Alec realised that things were going well, he fell into one of his bad, old habits. He immediately jumped to the negative conclusion that his good play couldn't last and everything would soon fall apart! His thinking changed from a positive relaxed approach to a negative approach.

Alec knew from experience that when his thinking became negative, he would start trying to 'prevent something bad happening' and his play would become defensive. This then made him tense and anxious, causing him to try and steer or over-control his shots. The result was a 'self fulfilling prophecy' – everything went horribly wrong!

A plan for Alec

Alec set out to overcome this problem by using several of the Basic Mental Skills. The plan he devised consisted of three parts:

1. He decided to set himself some performance-related goals[1] rather than the outcome goals he had subconsciously been using. Alec had always assumed that winning was the only gain or benefit to be had from playing golf. This outcome goal put him under pressure because it gave him a 'fear of losing'.

Alec chose his performance goal by analysing his game to identify his major weaknesses. He soon realised that his chipping was letting him down badly. When he missed a green, he usually only got close enough for a tap-in about once in every ten attempts! Therefore, he set a target of getting 'up and down' on three out of every five occasions. This would be achieved by first reaching the interim targets of '1 in 5' and '2 in 5'. He looked forward to the improvement in his scoring that meeting these targets would bring.

2. Having read the section on building self confidence[2] Alec resolved to stop attributing a good run of play to luck and believing that it must run out. He also started to give himself and his technique credit when he was scoring well.

3. The idea of developing some positive self statements[3] to use when he was playing was the final part of Alec's plan. By repeating to himself statements such as "I'm playing OK because I'm relaxed and enjoying this – I will stay relaxed and keep it going" Alec allowed less room for negativity to creep in and spoil his performance.

Alec's performance goals reduced the anxiety created by the 'fear of losing' because he knew that even if he lost there was the opportunity to gain a sense of achievement from reaching a personal goal. Together with his increased self belief Alec is now ready and confident to meet the challenge of keeping a good round going. He no longer fears losing because he knows each round is not 'life or death' but a stepping-stone towards making himself a better player.

References:

1. pages 42–44
2. pages 63–67
3. pages 32–34

2
THIS NEEDS 101%

Come on... This is vital... You have got to give this one hundred and one per cent... Concentrate, concentrate... The thoughts raced through Bill's mind as he addressed the putt.

Bill shuffled his feet again and finally hit the ball. The ball raced past the hole, it was always going to be too hard.

'Bad luck,' grinned his opponent. 'Your turn to win the next time.'

Bill had wanted to win so badly and he had tried so hard. No one could say he had lost for lack of trying! In fact his friends were always saying that he tried too hard. *Maybe they are right...* mused Bill afterwards, but how can anyone try too hard? *Surely that is the best way to ensure you concentrate on what you are doing....*

Is Bill right, or is there a better way for him to approach the game?

You can try too hard . . .

Rumour has it that all of Bill's end of year school reports contained the cryptic sentence – 'Bill is trying'. And, bless him, he is still trying. He is trying to be a good friend, a terrific dad, a perfect husband. He is trying very hard to be a great success at his job, as well as trying to be the best at all his interests – especially golf. What is more, he is succeeding... Bill can indeed be very trying!

Unfortunately, Bill has made the very common error of confusing 'trying' with 'persistence' and 'effort'. He believes that people who don't seem to 'try' are idle, inferior and don't care about things. Therefore, since he cares passionately about his golf, then he must 'try' his utmost to win and be seen to be trying. Bill's idea of trying is to give every task 101% physical and mental effort. So, for example, his tee shots resemble the efforts of an Olympic hammer thrower! He addresses the ball with every muscle and sinew tightened almost to breaking point. His jaw is set and teeth clenched so the veins stand out on his forehead. His knuckles gleam white as he grips the club with rubber-melting ferocity. He knows a little about visualisation and focusing, so sets his mind to what he calls a 'positive' thought, that is to say, trying to picture the ball flying 300 yards down the middle! As he is about to swing he stares unblinkingly at the back of the ball, willing it to the hole, then concentrates fiercely on his swing, forcing himself to remember every little technical detail he has learned.

In spite of all this effort, Bill's golf does not improve. His 'trying' makes him too tense to play consistently. He needs to change his approach to the game.

This will not be easy!

Helping Bill was not an easy task! For a start he was unable to understand the notion of 'not trying so hard' – how on earth can you improve your golf by not trying so hard? Another thing is that anything you suggest for him to do – like 'not try so hard' – he of course tries very hard at! The suggestions we had for Bill were a mixture of changing some of his thinking and changing the way he did things. In the past he had been given all sorts of suggestions, including taking a large brandy or smoking dope before a match! Here are some of the things we suggested all of which we hope are legal, decent and honest!

Because he was always 'trying' to achieve something, Bill's focus of attention[1] was very external. As a result he was not aware that there was any difference in his muscle tension or strength of grip between when he was engaged in competitive play and when he was more relaxed, for example on the practice ground. We suggested that when practising and not under pressure he focus his attention inward and become aware of what his grip 'feels' like, what his muscles 'feel' like and what his body is doing. This needs to be repeated many times to imprint that 'feeling' in the mind. Then, when playing under pressure, he can focus inward and check to see if his grip and muscles 'feel' right.

It was pointed out to Bill that it was the 'trying' that was interfering with his swing. We suggested that as an experiment he could adopt a different approach for a few weeks. If it didn't work then he could go back to 'trying'. We suggested that Bill imagine that he didn't particularly care about winning a game of golf, and to consider what that would look like and how he would act and then to actually play or act 'as – if' this were the case. So, for example, when playing a tee shot, he should not put much effort in to the swing and, if anything, aim to drop the ball short of his normal distance. When putting he should imagine that the aim is not to bother too much about holing out, whilst not making it look too much like that is what he is doing. If Bill can manage to do this for several rounds, it is hoped that he will see that when he is not 'trying' so hard his game does not deteriorate. In fact, his consistency will probably improve!

Bill had a good steady rhythm in his practice swing, but when he stepped up to hit the ball his forward swing became an unbalanced and violent hack at the ball. We advised him to work on a new swing thought.[2] Our suggestion was to think not of 'hitting' the ball, but of 'making a practice swing' and the ball just happens to get in the way!

References:

1. pages 45–48
2. pages 54–55

3 DEREK'S BETTER ON HIS OWN!

'I play some of my best golf when I am on my own,' moaned Derek one evening as he emerged from the gloom into the welcoming warmth of the nineteenth hole. 'I think it is because I can play the shots in my own time without anyone rushing me, and I don't feel any pressure,' he explained to his friends in the bar.

'Do you beat yourself often then?' joked one of his pals.

'If I could play the way I did this evening on a regular basis, I would beat you every time,' snapped Derek. 'And without any strokes either.'

Could Derek play as well in a competition as he does when on his own? Why is there such a difference in the two situations?

Golf's classic dilemma

In many ways Derek's case is a perfect example of why playing golf is at least 50% 'between the ears'. In fact, Derek's problem is just what happens to all of us to a greater or lesser extent. Technically, Derek can play excellent golf. This is most evident when he is relaxed, for example playing on his own, or when he is on the practice range. In a competition, however, he becomes tense and his game goes to pieces.

Derek's technical ability is the result of regular practice. The one thing he does not practise, though, is handling pressure! This is why there is such a difference in the two situations. Derek does not lack confidence in his abilities as a golfer, but he lacks confidence in his ability to handle himself under pressure. So, when there is pressure on him in a competitive round, he easily becomes tense and plays badly.

What Derek should try

Derek needs to develop strategies to slowly build confidence in his ability to handle pressure. He should try using imagery[1] so that when he is practising he can put himself under pressure by imagining he is playing in a competition. He could also put pressure on himself by limiting the time he has to play each shot. In this way he can slowly get used to playing under pressure.

A particularly useful skill for him to learn would be a good relaxation technique.[2] By developing this, he would have a relaxation trigger on hand to quickly control the tension that builds up before playing a shot. Just knowing that he can do this will give him confidence in his ability to handle pressure.

Finally Derek should keep reminding himself that he can play well when not under pressure so all he has to do is handle the pressure and soon he will be able to wipe the smile off the faces of his tormentors in the 19th!

References:

1. pages 24–28
2. pages 17–19

4 DISASTER IS ALWAYS ROUND THE CORNER...

'It's really stupid, but I always seem to do it,' explained Lucy. 'Take today for example. I started with four straight pars and when I stood on the fifth tee, I thought to myself... be prepared because this is sure to be a bad hole. It wasn't, and I managed another par! However, I had the same thoughts again on the sixth tee... be ready, because this time it will be a disaster. Again it wasn't – another par! On the seventh tee I just knew it was all going to go wrong... and this time it did. My luck ran out. I took seven and my whole game collapsed.'

Her long-time partner Angela consoled her. 'You're capable of playing to a much lower handicap than twelve. Just be patient. One day it will all come together and you will shoot eighteen pars. Wait and see.'

Should Lucy 'wait and see', or is there something she can do to improve her mental approach?

It's all down to luck!

Lucy had always been rather a shy girl and had lacked belief in herself all her life. She could remember at school that she quite enjoyed sport, especially hockey. Her enjoyment was often spoiled, though, by a rather cruel sports teacher who liked to pick on shy girls. Lucy can remember that whatever she did in a hockey game was discounted in some way. If she played a good shot, it was labelled as lucky or chance, and as a game wore on she would become disheartened and her playing would deteriorate. She had no belief in the idea that she might have any skill, or that she was making an effort, and since anything she did well was 'only down to luck', she felt no sense of achievement or pleasure from a game.

Lucy still holds those beliefs and, as all luck is finite, she knows it must run out at some point. Luck is out of our control and if we have no real skill or ability then we cannot play well for long. So, when Lucy plays golf, she attributes any good shots purely to luck, which must run out eventually. After playing well for a few holes, if she hits a bad shot, she interprets that as being proof that the good shots were due to luck. She cannot control luck, therefore there is nothing she can do. She then becomes overwhelmed by negativity, becomes disheartened and her game disintegrates.

When Angela, Lucy's friend, said 'wait and see', she was already devising a scheme to help Lucy. Angela had recently been to a *Golf Between the Ears* training workshop and had learned about the importance of effective attribution.[1] It was clear that Lucy had the unhelpful thinking habit of attributing any golf success to luck rather than skill, concentration and effort. From the workshop, Angela knew that this was an unhelpful habit that could be changed.

Lucy's guardian angel lends a hand

Angela had to find a way to show Lucy that by believing that when she was making par on a hole it was because she was doing all the right things, like staying relaxed, focused and using her shot routines – not because of 'luck'. Similarly, if she hit a bad shot it was because of something she had failed to control, like allowing negative thoughts to creep into her mind.

Angela determined to live up to her name and become Lucy's angel. So, the following weekend, as they were in the locker room getting ready to play, Angela looked over to where Lucy was tying up the laces on her golf shoes and said, 'You are the luckiest person I've ever seen, Lucy.'

'What do you mean?' was the puzzled reply.

'Well, you always seem to tie a really good double bow on both your shoe laces.'

Lucy moved closer to Angela and sniffed her breath, checking for the tell-tale whiff of gin, known to be Angela's favourite tipple. Unmoved, Angela pressed on.

'You seem to have a hundred percent good luck, because sure as golf balls are golf balls, there you are, every week, two perfectly tied shoe laces.'

'I'm getting seriously worried about you Angela. What has luck got to do with tying shoe laces?'

'Well, how else do you explain the fact that you do that so well every week?' replied Angela matter-of-factly.

'Because I learned to do it a long time ago. I've done it many times since and I pay attention to what I am doing – and just how do you hide the smell of gin on your breath?'

Angela was undaunted. 'But surely, Lucy, you must sometimes think or worry that you might not get your laces tied properly – don't you ever think that the good run of lace tying must end sometime?"

'Listen "gin-head," I might fumble a bit when my fingers are cold, or I'm rushing, and they might not always be the same tightness or as tight as I would like them, but I never for one minute doubt that I won't get them tied up. I know how to do it – *there is no luck involved in tying shoe laces!*'

'But there is in swinging a golf club . . . ?'

'What? Well, that's different.'

'How so?'

'Because . . . because . . . well, it just is!'

Angela knew that she had sown the seeds of change in Lucy's mind. Lucy started to understand that if she shot par, it was down to her, not luck. Similarly, when she hit a bad shot it was because of some reason over which she has control such as focusing or tension. Once she had grasped that, then she could learn to accept a bad shot as just that, not a slice of bad luck, and consequently she does not have to let her game go to pieces. Lucy never doubts she can tie her shoe laces so she succeeds at doing this because she believes she has control – *she can do that with her golf.*

Even if it exists, the amount of luck involved in the mechanics of a golf swing is minute. Is there really any more luck involved in hitting a golf shot to the best of your ability than tying up your golf shoes?

References:

1. pages 56–62

5   WHEN THE RED MIST COMES DOON ...

Hammy was having another bad day! It all began at the sixth when he missed a short putt and sent his putter whistling through the air towards the next tee. He was still fuming when his fourball reached the eleventh. Hammy's hooked drive into the pond was followed by another exhibition of his club throwing skills. This time he narrowly missed one of his partners. 'That's it,' warned Derek, his long-suffering partner. 'If you throw one more club I will never play with you again.'

'Same goes for us,' chimed in his opponents.

Hammy managed to keep his temper under control for the rest of the round. He was annoyed with himself, embarrassed by his behaviour, and worried at the prospect of being ostracised by his friends. He also recognised that his game suffered when he lost his cool. Hammy didn't like his club throwing antics but 'When the red mist comes doon', as he described it, he was unable to stop himself; he felt he was going to explode unless he took his frustration out on the offending implement!

Hammy knew he must find a way of keeping himself in check...

Don't get angry at yourself

As you can see, Hammy has a big temper, but he also has a big heart and can be a very loyal friend. It may be several hundred years since an ancestor of Hammy's fought for the honour of the family name, but the blood of the proud Highland warrior courses through his veins. To this day he hears his father's voice telling him that: 'A real man keeps his pride by defending his honour from every threat.' The problem is that he often sees a threat where there is none. In particular, he sees anything bad that he does as a threat to his pride and so gets very angry with himself.

Golf is important to Hammy, so if he plays a bad shot he believes he is letting himself down. People have even heard him muttering to himself, 'Pull yourself together, you should be ashamed of yourself, you're a disgrace.' The angrier he becomes with himself, the more tense he becomes and the less he is able to focus. As his game deteriorates, he is almost screaming at himself. Eventually, as he is about to explode, he lets off steam, usually by throwing a club!

The red mist clears

After this particular game, Hammy sloped off to the 19th for a calming drink and we were fortunate enough to overhear a conversation that ensued. He was still tense and 'wound up' following his outbursts on the course.

'You're going to spill that before you manage to drink it,' observed Jimmy the club barman. 'Anyway, drink isn't the answer.'

'Ach, away wi yersel', richt noo it's the best answer I've got. And when people like you, Jimmy, leave me be tae get it doon ma throat, it works!'

Jimmy was unperturbed. 'You know what? I reckon you must be one of those "skitso-maniacs", or whatever they're called.'

'A whit?' blustered Hammy, his blood beginning to boil again.

'You know, like you're two different people. I've seen you out there coaching the kids from the junior team. When one of them hits a bad shot, you don't go raving mad shouting at them, or anything like that.'

'Well, ma pride is no at stake wi' them playin',' retorted Hammy.

'Don't give me that rubbish. Those kids are all as important to you as if they were your own. What's more, you're their coach. If they play badly in a competition, it surely reflects on you?'

'Aye, you may be right, Jimmy, but you canna go gettin' mad at the bairns. They try awfy hard, and if I shouted at them they'd get upset, disheartened and maybe go off in a huff. You hae tae be firm but fair. Be encouragin', nurturin' and motivatin', that's why they're a' doin' sae well.'

'Like I said, you're two different people, encouraging and motivating the kids, even when they make a mistake, but ripping yourself to pieces if you're less than perfect. Why do you coach yourself differently from the way you coach the kids?'

'Cos they're bairns and I'm old enough to know better. Another large Scotch while you're at it.'

'Huh! And you think that because you're old enough to drink whisky that under that big ugly exterior there might not be a "kid" that would respond well to being encouraged and motivated, rather than being yelled at?'

Now Jimmy had a point there! We know that strong emotions, particularly anger at ourselves, are a block to playing golf to the best of our abilities. Hammy believes that 'letting off steam' is good for him, as he thinks it releases his frustration. He may *feel* that, but it is definitely not the recommended way of reducing tension! By getting so worked up, Hammy will have raised the tension in his body to fever pitch, and as this will take a long time to subside, it will hinder his playing of the remaining holes. Getting angry is a habitual response for some people like Hammy, and the best way to stop throwing clubs is to not get angry in the first place!

Hammy can certainly reduce his anger in several ways. He needs to change the way he talks to himself, and 'coach' himself as he does the kids in the Junior team, just as Jimmy suggested. Hammy would also do well to read the section on changing his thinking[1] as he certainly sees threats where there are none, and his reaction is naturally to react with anger. For example, if he plays a bad shot he will think something like... *You stupid idiot. You're just humiliating yourself in front of other people*... Of course, if someone else had said that to Hammy, he would have become very angry with them; similarly when he thinks that about himself, he becomes angry with himself. After studying the section on thinking skills[1] Hammy changed this thought to: 'That was not a great shot, but that's all it is – a poor shot; it does not mean anything bad about me.' Hammy should also learn to regulate his anger by becoming more aware of the early warning signals and then reducing his anger with relaxation[2] and calming self-statements[3] such as, 'Anger is tension and that could affect my play – relax and stay cool.'

References:

1. pages 22–23
2. pages 17–18
3. pages 32–35

6

I KNEW I WAS GOING TO DO THAT...

Nick's mind was working overtime, *You can't miss this putt...It's only four feet...It is dead straight, slightly uphill...The only thing you could do wrong is not hit it hard enough....* The putt finished short, hanging over the lip of the hole.

'I knew I was going to do that,' cried Nick. 'I just knew it. I talked myself out of it. I couldn't get the feeling of knocking it in. The dominant message in my mind and the feeling I had in my hands was of decelerating the putter and not hitting the putt hard enough. And that is exactly what I did! If I could get the same strong feeling that I was going to make a positive stroke rather than always feeling a negative one, I am sure I would hole loads more putts.'

'That's why we are not scratch men,' observed Paul, his long-suffering partner. 'We play so many bad shots that is what our mind and muscles know best. We can't expect to be positive. I always have negative thoughts on the tee, where the only thought or feeling I can generate is that of a bad drive heading into trouble.'

Is Paul correct, or can he and Nick generate some positive images?

Negativity is a habit

'Negative Nick' and 'Pessimistic Paul' – what a pair! The Nicks of this world are usually negative about everything, from the weather to the economy and from the state of the golf course to the state of their own game. Consequently, they have little experience or skill at thinking more realistically and positively, or generating effective positive images. Their minds always revert to the 'default setting' of negativity.

Negativity is pervasive, and human beings have evolved to be particularly sensitive to negativity. When you think negatively it de-motivates, interferes with your mental and physical skills, and saps your energy. Basically, being negative does not have anything going for it. Unfortunately, negativity is a habit that anyone can easily slip in to . . .

Can Nick and Paul learn to generate positive images?

The answer is 'yes', but to succeed requires a great deal of work, effort and a *sustained attack on negativity*. Paul and Nick must first decide that they want to be more positive. We had to first of all get them to relinquish the negativity, so we asked them if being negative worked. The answer of course was 'no'. We then had to develop a programme to retrain them to habitually think in a more realistic and positive manner.

Thinking positively seems to be easier for some people than others. This may be because of their particular circumstances, or because they have a natural predisposition towards optimism. But whatever our circumstances may be, we all have a choice as to the attitude we take to any given situation. Every morning you wake up you can choose to make the effort to think positively and make the best of any circumstances. Similarly with your golf, you can choose to make the effort to think about your play realistically, to work at positive self statements[1] and to work at learning effective imagery skills.[2] The 'Between the Ears' team drew up the following seven-point plan for Nick and Paul which included elements designed to repeat and rehearse positive mental experiences:

1. All negative talk or criticism of their play is banned, especially immediately after a game. Only positive aspects of the game are to be discussed.
2. When they hit a good shot, immediately try to repeat the swing and go through the shot mentally to try 'seeing' it and 'feeling' it.

3. Away from the course sit and relax (use relaxation skills[3]) and try to 'picture' and 'feel' recent good shots. This is best done soon after playing and should be repeated on a regular basis. It needn't take more than ten minutes! Try and include this exercise in physical practice sessions.

4. After hitting a bad shot, do not repeat the swing. Briefly tense and relax the muscles or shake the body to remove the 'feeling' of the shot. Do not engage emotionally with the shot – imagine you have just watched someone else play the shot and *briefly* observe what was not good about the shot, for example, 'that shot was hooked'. Only engage in 'why' when on the practice range.

5. Learn and practise positive statements, which must be used after a good shot, for example, 'That felt good – I was relaxed and focused', and after a bad shot, for example, 'That was not where I would have liked the ball to go but I have learned and I will enjoy the challenge of still trying to make par.'

6. Away from the course, practise developing positive imagery[4] to include in the shot routine.

7. Create a relaxation trigger.[5] It is easier to engage in positive imagery when you are relaxed and the mind is still.

So, if in the next few months you happen to drop in to the bar at the Dizzy Heights Golf Club and bump in to a couple of cheerful easy-going young guys who excitedly talk about their rapidly decreasing handicaps; it might just be 'Positive Paul' and the 'No Longer Negative Nick'!

References:

1. pages 33–34
2. pages 24–28
3. pages 17–19
4. page 28
5. pages 139–144

7 STEVE DOESN'T 'GIVE IT A GO' ANY LONGER

Steve is an aggressive golfer who loves to, as he says, 'Give it a go'. He is a bit cocky and over confident, especially on the greens where he is famed for 'rattling in' the difficult putts. Steve doesn't mind having a long one back if he misses – he knows he'll hole it!

One Sunday, Steve and his partner Ian came to the last green all square in the final of the club four-ball tournament. Ian had picked up and Steve was left with a ten-footer for a birdie and the match. Steve, as usual, went for the putt, just missed and went three feet past. His relieved opponents, like the members watching round the green, fully expected Steve would, as usual, hole the return putt. But to their and Steve's amazement he missed, losing the match.

Steve has never been the same man since. He has lost all confidence, his boldness has gone. As Steve says himself: 'I'm terrified of hitting it past the hole in case I have a tricky one back. Instead, I leave a tricky one by being short! I am now happy to lay it dead from ten feet'.

What has gone wrong in Steve's mind? Should he try and become an aggressive putter again, or should he take a different approach?

Understanding Steve's problem

To make sense of Steve's problem, it is helpful to understand what happened and why. There are two fundamental ways to develop self confidence. Firstly, having realistically positive and constructive ways of thinking about things, and secondly, experiencing successful performances. Steve's confidence was a result of the latter. He was used to success, his belief in his ability was so strong that he always played to his best, or in his words, he wasn't afraid to 'give it a go'. His confidence in this approach was based on a great deal of success. Of course he had missed his fair share of putts, but none of them had been that important. He had no experience of coping with major setbacks or missing important shots.

When Steve three putted, missing the short return putt, to lose in front of so many people, he felt shattered and was unable to deal with the apparent destruction of the belief in himself. He felt his reputation as a great putter was in ruins. He even began to believe the old adage, 'Success seems to happen in private, but spectacular failure always seems to happen in full view'.

Because he felt so 'awful' about missing the putt and losing the match, he is afraid of feeling like that again, and subconsciously tries to avoid leaving himself any tricky short putts.

Getting Steve's confidence back

Most of the techniques which Steve needs to rebuild his confidence are described in the section 'Building Confidence'.[1] He should particularly try to:

1. Change the way he talks to himself. He has a tendency to say to himself that losing or making a mistake is 'awful' and 'intolerable'. As a result, he gets tense and anxious, which is no good for successful putting! He should talk to himself in a more encouraging way, for example, 'Missing a putt is one stroke, not the end of the world', 'I putted well because I believed I could. My ability to putt can't have just disappeared. It's only my belief that I've lost and I will get that back'.

2. Remember that he played well when he acted confidently. He could experiment by acting 'as if' he were confident again, even if at first he doesn't feel like pretending.

3. Take every opportunity to 'own up to' his mistakes[2] so that he learns

to tolerate the feelings of a poor performance, and become less afraid of those feelings. As he does this, his confidence will return as a result of ceasing to be afraid of failure.

References:

1. pages 63–67
2. pages 59–62

8

I ALWAYS FEEL I'M RUSHING...

'Have you got a torch in case you don't finish before dark?' The remark came out of the crowd standing around the first tee and everyone roared with laughter. Phil, a low handicapper, was marked out as a slow player and everyone loved to make jokes at his expense.

Phil had tried speeding up, but he found this made him hit more bad shots than when he waited until he was ready to play his shot. If Phil could take the shots in his own time, he played to scratch easily, but he always felt rushed and had to grind out his score by scrambling with chips and putts.

These remarks and his reputation for slowness put his mind in terrible turmoil. He couldn't play more quickly, because then he only played worse. If he tried to convince himself to ignore the outside influences and take the time he needed, he seemed to take even longer! His mind kept telling him, *People are waiting...the group behind are timing you...* and this stopped him concentrating on his shots. Phil had resigned himself to playing under this strain, but after so many years it was making him think about giving the game up!

Should Phil give up, or can he make himself a quicker player without feeling he's being rushed?

It depends on your habits!

Phil really has reached a crossroads – although it took him ages to get there! No, seriously, enough jokes at his expense. The fact is everyone plays at a different speed depending on the various habits that they have developed over the years. These habits will develop as a result of thoughts and fears a player has, such as 'hitting a bad shot will be totally humiliating', as well as from repeating initially successful techniques, like taking a long time to 'feel' right about a putt. For players at the extremes, that is to say, either very fast or very slow, there will always be problems. Fast players can see their game fall apart when they start to become frustrated by playing against a slow opponent, or when they are held up by slow players in front of them. Similarly, when poor old Phil tries to speed up, he plays badly because he feels hustled, anxious and tense.

Phil faces up to the problem

The first thing is for Phil to decide to either quit now or have a genuine shot at changing things. He resolved to 'have a go' at changing and made up his mind to give golf another year. If he was not playing better and enjoying his golf more after that time, then he would take up embroidery instead! With the help of the 'Between the Ears' team a plan was designed for the year.

Phil began by determining why other players thought he was slow. He discussed whether they thought he wasted time between shots, left his clubs in the wrong place, etc. and discovered that everyone thought it was the time he took over playing his shots which made him slow! It was decided therefore that Phil should set himself the specific goal[1] of returning to ask these same people in a year's time whether he had speeded up or not; and have the majority of them answer 'YES'. Because this was a goal that Phil set for himself, he is more likely to succeed. What is more, because he asked people for their opinions of his game, he was able to accept their views as constructive criticism – not a 'put down'.

OK, so that is Phil's main goal, but to achieve a goal you must have a plan of action and intermediate goals.[1] Normally Phil would spend several minutes settling, sometimes even walking away from the ball, going to his bag and selecting another club before trying to settle again! So Phil decided one of his intermediate goals should be to complete a shot within one minute of it being his turn to play. To achieve this he developed a shot routine[2] round this time limit which he would practise and use consistently. This routine included focusing skills to help him switch into his routine quickly and effectively. He also worked on some of his negative thinking, and learned a set of positive self statements[3] that rid his mind of the doubt that caused him to change clubs several times. For example, part of his shot routine was to consider the shot to play and then select the club. Whereas, in the past, he would then start to have thoughts like 'I hope this is the right club, what if it's not?', he replaced that with a rule that once selected he would *not* change the club and repeated in his mind thoughts like, 'My choice of club is always good, this is the right club for the shot I want. If I stay relaxed and go through my shot routine the result will be fine.'

Phil set similar goals for tackling his putting routine, which everyone saw as painfully slow. By making gradual improvements in the speed of various aspects of his game, Phil will increase the overall speed of his game without affecting the standard. In fact, he may well play better as he won't feel hustled and anxious so often. He will feel confident that he is playing at a reasonable pace and cannot be criticised. And once people start agreeing he is playing more quickly, anyone who doesn't like it can go . . . .

References:

1. pages 41–44
2. pages 51–53
3. pages 32–34

9 | JANIE HAS A THING ABOUT BUNKERS

Janie is new to golf, having started just over two years ago. She has learned most of the shots to some degree, apart from getting out of sand bunkers, which is her Achilles Heel. She still hasn't entered a medal competition because of her fear of bunkers. Once she is in one she is in – permanently! Until she picks up her ball and climbs out!

The professional has given her many lessons, and she can play the shot when he is talking her through it. However, out on the course she just goes to pieces. 'All I can see are bunkers,' she says. 'I am in a state of panic all the way round in case my ball goes in one – which it inevitably does.'

Janie is currently looking for a course with no sand bunkers! But is there some way she could overcome this mental block?

Mountaineers don't look for molehills!

Looking for a course with no bunkers will obviously not solve Janie's problem. Maybe she could also look for one with wider fairways and holes 3 feet across!

Let us step back for a moment and ask ourselves a fundamental question. Do we not play golf for the challenge it presents – the challenge of golfer against the course? Like mountaineers who constantly look for ever more difficult mountains to climb, there is huge satisfaction in overcoming the difficulties in front of us. But we never hear of mountaineers looking for molehills to climb so they can say they reached the top!

The satisfaction of golf surely lies in overcoming our fears and frailties to master the course or our opponent – no matter how difficult! This is what Janie needs to recognise if she is going to overcome her mental block.

So what does all this mean for Janie?

First Janie must consider her goals. She must decide that her aims are **to overcome whatever difficulties there are on the golf course**. She could make this aim into a positive statement[1] and repeat it to herself. Having got herself into a negative 'mindset' about bunkers, Janie has convinced herself that she cannot cope with them, and that they are something to be feared and avoided. To counteract this, she should construct some more positive statements to help her cope. For example, when she is about to tee off she might be thinking *I hope I don't end up in a bunker – but I probably will*, but she can counter this by saying to herself, *There is a lot more fairway than sand out there, but if I did happen to end up in a bunker that is OK because it will be a chance to practise my recovery technique.*

If she does go in to a bunker, rather than thinking *Oh no, what a disaster, I'm going to be stuck in here for ever,* she should replace that thought with, *Good! I've been practising for this with the pro. It's an opportunity to test my new skills under pressure.*

Janie should also ensure she has a routine[2] for bunker shots which must be exactly the same whether it is a practice session or a competitive round. She could try including some strong imagery[3] that includes 'visualising' and 'hearing' the pro talking her through the shot even when he is not there.

Lastly, Janie must confront her fear head on. Fear is like a rainbow. If you walk towards a rainbow it seems to get further away from you. The same happens with fears. When you go towards them they recede and then disappear. If Janie played a round of golf deliberately trying to put herself in every bunker – she might actually find it quite difficult!

References:

1. pages 29–31
2. pages 51–53
3. pages 24–28

IO

WISE AFTER THE EVENT

'If only I could have that shot over again,' bemoaned Colin, 'I would play it brilliantly this time.' His partners roared with laughter, reminding him that in golf you don't get a second chance.

Colin knew that only too well, but he got very annoyed within himself. Colin had trouble settling his mind to the shot in hand. He found it difficult to get a 'good swing thought' for some shots and so feel confident about playing them. However, if he played the shot badly, immediately afterwards a 'clear picture' of the shot crystallised in his mind and he felt totally confident about playing it properly if given a second chance. This process occurred so often that Colin was convinced he could avoid these bad shots if he could remove the mental block and get that 'clear picture' first time around.

Why does Colin have to hit the shot badly to get the good 'feeling' that now he can play the exact same shot well? Can he reverse the process?

Tension is the problem

We all know it's easy to be 'wise after the event', especially Colin! On the face of it, Colin's problem may seem a bit of a mystery. He does, after all, seem to have most mental skills in place. He is able to visualise clearly the shot and can even 'feel' the required shot. Unfortunately, this picture is strongest in his mind after he has hit a poor shot. So, why are his visualisation skills at their best 'after the event'?

As discussed in the Basic Mental Skills, you will play your best golf when you are not *too* keyed up. When you are reasonably calm and relaxed you will have better access to your mental and physical skills. Because his golf has always been important to him, Colin is probably getting too 'psyched up', and this has become a block preventing him from getting his thinking skills working properly on every shot.

After he hits a bad shot there will be a release of all the tension, which caused the mishit, making Colin's mind and body more relaxed. Being calmer and less tense therefore allows Colin's mental skills to be used more effectively and the 'picture' of the shot he wanted to play becomes clear in his mind.

So, how do we help Colin?

As we can see, Colin's visualisation skills are fine, he had worked very hard to develop them, but he needs to 'cool it' a bit. He must reduce tension, in order to access these skills, at their peak, as and when required – not after he has hit one 'Out of Bounds'! A little time devoted to improving his relaxation skills[1] and finding a way to calm himself mentally and physically before playing a shot will go a long way to achieving this. A suggestion might be to practise a relaxation technique,[2] during which, he repeats the word 'calm' as he breathes out. After several weeks practising this away from the course, he will associate breathing slowly and deeply and repeating 'calm', in his mind, with a feeling of relaxation. Then, before hitting a shot, he can do this and relax his mind and body enough to access his shot routine and visualisation skills.

Colin's case is interesting because it shows that you must develop a range of mental skills for golf. Some of the skills, like the relaxation 'trigger' will help you make better use of other skills such as visualisation and focusing.

References:

1. pages 17–19
2. pages 139–144

11   WHAT'S THAT SOUND?

Doug was taking his final waggle prior to hitting his opening drive in his match against the aptly nicknamed 'Major Upset'. Doug hesitated, *What was that noise? Sounds like someone rattling their loose change...* he said to himself, standing away from the ball. The noise ceased and Doug settled down over the ball once more. *There it is again... just as I was about to hit the ball,* thought Doug; *it's definitely deliberate.*

Doug decided to confront the Major. 'I know you're trying to put me off. Please stop rattling your change.'

'Nothing of the kind, old boy,' retorted the Major. 'Hope you are not going to be as touchy as this all the way round. Anyway, I don't mind a bit of needle in the game if that's the way you want it.'

I wish I hadn't said anything, thought Doug, feeling the tension rising in his muscles.

The rest of the round was a nightmare for Doug, who was totally on edge. *I shouldn't have confronted him... It just made me tighten up... and unable to relax and concentrate,* thought Doug to himself as he trudged up the hill to the clubhouse, having lost comfortably by 5 and 4.

Should Doug have challenged the Major or should he have said nothing?

No easy answer to Doug's dilemma!

The etiquette of golf is quite clear about being silent whilst someone is playing a shot. However, we will often come across golfers who are perhaps a bit noisy or distracting, but this is usually because they are not really aware of what they are doing, or just being careless. These players can normally be reasoned with to moderate their behaviour and so avoid distractions. Regrettably, every now and then we will meet someone like the Major who is pompous, arrogant and does not give a jot about anyone. Basically he doesn't care how he wins and sees nothing wrong in a bit of what he calls 'gamesmanship'.

The best course of action, when faced with Doug's situation, has to be considered by weighing the 'cost' of such action against the potential 'gain'. For example, some people may have been tempted to play the Major at his own game and try and distract him when he takes a shot. But bear in mind that the Major has played these sorts of tricks most of his life. He is very good at it. Playing him at his own game may end up with a total loss of your concentration! On the other hand, confronting the situation as Doug did may leave you feeling uncomfortable, unsettled and with your concentration broken once again. Everyone has to decide on what is the best course of action for themselves as individuals. This will usually be the one with which they feel most comfortable. Preparing oneself for such situations is therefore important.

So for poor old Doug, who was totally unprepared, there was no right answer. No matter what he did, including doing nothing at all, there was always going to be the potential for distraction and loss of concentration!

Preparing for the next time...

Doug must ask himself whether doing nothing and trying to ignore the distractions is an option. If he feels comfortable that he can maintain his concentration and focus, despite the deliberate distractions, then he should choose this course of action. If not, then he should decide what he would like to happen the next time, and assertively stick up for his rights. Every golfer has the right to expect fair and sporting conduct from an opponent.

Many people, like Doug, are hesitant to stick up for themselves because they think they will be labelled a 'whinger'. The attitudes we adopt in certain situations are a habit and these can be changed by questioning whether our current attitude[1] is helpful or not in improving the situation. Doug does this and comes to the conclusion that the Major is just a bully, and probably behaves this way to everyone, and if he stands up to him other club members will probably rally behind him.

To achieve this, Doug should first state clearly and assertively what he expects the Major to do and what action he plans to take if the Major doesn't do it! For example he could say – 'I believe what you are doing is a deliberate attempt to distract me and, if you persist, I will withdraw from the game and lodge an official complaint with the club secretary.'

Doug knows the Major is good at this game and will try to discount his complaint and belittle him in any way possible. Also, if Doug engaged him in debate he may lose. So, the answer is to use a technique often called the 'broken record', where you just repeat pretty much the same thing over and over again without engaging in an argument. Doug should therefore repeat the statement he made above to prevent being forced into a discussion by the Major. This course of action may be tough and Doug should be prepared to follow through with what he has said. Usually, however, if you stand up to bullies in a confident and assertive way, they will back down.

Knowing that this is his chosen course of action and feeling comfortable with it should mean that the possibility of Doug being distracted is greatly reduced. Doug might also employ some positive self-talk[2] to help him through. This could be along the lines of, 'I am in the right, and my actions are totally justified. I am comfortable and at peace with this course of action.'

Most golfers are all too familiar with deliberate gamesmanship. Being prepared for such an encounter will make you confident about being able to handle the situation without it causing total disaster for your own game. You never know, you might visit Dizzy Heights and be the first golfer to rattle the Major and make him back down!

References:

1. pages 22–23
2. pages 32–34

12 THE 'BOGEY HOLE'

'Was that a nine?' enquired Pam's partner as they left the tenth green. Pam was so annoyed she didn't want to answer.

'Yes, yes,' she finally agreed. 'I don't think I've ever played that blasted hole decently in my whole life. Whoever designed it was a sadist!'

Pam's frustration was understandable. Before she had arrived at the club to play this Medal round, she had been worrying about how she was going to play this particular hole. Thoughts of her impending doom at this, her 'bogey hole', had even kept her awake the night before. And here was the reality come true . . . As predicted, another disaster at the tenth.

'Imagine it's just another hole,' consoled her partner.

That's easy for you to say, thought Pam as she tore up her card and threw it in the bin.

Can Pam overcome this mental block about the tenth hole?

Analysing the mental block

Pam can definitely overcome her mental block at the tenth so long as she understands that is what it is – a mental block! What seems to be preventing her from playing to the best of her ability at this hole is her:

☐ **Motivation** (or rather – lack of motivation) towards fixing the problem. Pam always tried to not think about the tenth hole before a game, a strategy that actually made her worry about it even more!

Whilst playing she would 'try' to get past it as quickly as possible and, after the game, would 'try' and put it out of her mind – all strategies which failed! She felt no energy or motivation towards finding a better way to cope with the hole – she just wanted to forget it as soon as possible! As she avoided dealing with the problem her difficulties persisted.

◻ **Attitude** to the hole. Aristotle recognised the problem, even before golf was invented, when he observed that, 'Whenever we hold the belief that something is terrible or fearsome, we at once experience the corresponding emotion . . . ' Unfortunately, Pam takes just this attitude!

◻ **Memories** of constant failure at the tenth. Pam only recalls how badly she felt and how humiliating it was whenever she played the hole. As a result she predicts that she will always play it poorly, which in turn becomes a 'self fulfilling prophecy'.

Pam can tame the tenth

Having broken the one big mental block down into the three smaller, more identifiable and manageable blocks outlined above, we suggested to Pam the following ways of overcoming each in turn:

◻ **Motivation** – As we have mentioned a number of other times in this book, just reading about and **knowing** the mental skills is not enough. You must have the motivation to put consistent **effort** in to using and practising the skills. Pam needed to find the necessary motivation to make the changes, as avoiding the problem had become such a habit. You might think that just wanting to play the hole better would motivate her, but we can all get stuck in the rut of just accepting a bad situation rather than dealing with it.

Pam's motivation came quite by chance. Whilst relating another poor performance at the tenth, Pam repeated her comment that whoever designed the hole must have been a sadist.

'Yes,' replied her partner, 'and you can guarantee it was a man!' Right there and then Pam found the motivation she needed. She had become quite successful in her job, which was in a very male-oriented business. Her success had often been achieved by overcoming the prejudices of her male colleagues. So, here was another example of a man standing in her way. It was 'a red rag to a bull'! A man had designed this golf course and she was not going to be beaten by him – no mere man was going to spoil her round of golf! She determined to do everything possible to overcome her difficulty with the tenth hole.

☐ **Attitude** – Having found the motivation and energy, Pam now had to improve her mental skills. The first step was to help her change her 'attitude'[1] to the hole. She had always called it her 'bogey hole' but changed this to the 'challenge hole'. This seemingly trivial change in the language we use can often bring about large changes in approach and effort. She sat down and 'argued' rationally with her-self that the **only** reason she played so badly at that particular hole was because she predicted she would. There was just no evidence that she **should** play it badly. Her golf skills weren't suddenly 'spir-ited' away as soon as she got to the tenth tee! In fact, there was every reason for Pam to do as well at that hole as at any other because it was not **technically more difficult** for her than any other. After this little debate with herself, she felt more positive about the hole and developed several positive statements[2] such as, 'Good, I'm looking forward to this challenge. I'll stay nice and relaxed and my skills will take me through,' to remind herself of her new attitude when next teeing off at the tenth.

☐ **Memories** – To help counter the numerous memories she had of playing the tenth badly, she developed a strong coping visualisation[3] of playing the hole. Sitting nice and relaxed in her armchair at home, she visualised herself playing the hole and maybe hitting a poor tee shot but recovering well to finish the hole in a one over par six, which was better than she usually played it. She ran this image through her mind at least two or three times a day. In these visualisations she saw herself recovering well from a range of not very good shots. Sometimes she ran the visualisation and saw herself play the hole well. This vivid imagery helped to counteract the negative memories, and give her a feeling that, even if she hit a poor shot, she could recover and not let the hole become a total disaster.

References:

1. pages 22–23
2. pages 32–34
3. pages 27–28

13   IS THERE A GOD OF GOLF?

Please let this be a good one...for once let me hit a boomer straight down the middle...please, please. Martin was praying to his imaginary god as he stood over his ball on the first tee. *With all these people watching...they will laugh and snigger at me if I hit a bad one...please for once let it sail down the middle.*

    The ball trickled off the tee into the deep rough just in front of the ladies tee. Some in the gallery stifled a laugh others turned away in embarrassment. Martin didn't look up. He picked up his tee, shouldered his bag and headed off to his ball. *It's always like this...* he thought.

    Does it always have to be like this or does Martin need to pray in a different way?

Believe in yourself

Yes, Martin does need to pray in a different way! By thinking the way he does, he clearly demonstrates that he has no confidence in the outcome of his shot and believes that he has no control over it. Martin has to start believing in himself and pray to the god 'Martin'! He must change his thinking to believe that he has control over what happens, and that he takes responsibility for the result, whether good or bad. Learning to use a strong visualisation of where he wants the shot to land would help to keep out the negativity of doubt.

What Martin needs to do

Martin obviously has a lot of work to do to improve his mental approach to the game. His thinking on that first tee was akin to a mild panic attack! Martin needs a little of all the Basic Mental Skills. However, to try and help him reduce those first tee nerves he should firstly concentrate his efforts on:

1. Developing his own 'relaxation trigger'[1] which he can use at any time to calm himself down. This will reduce the anxiety and tension, which are contributing to his poor shots.
2. Devising a shot routine,[2] which will help him focus on the shot and not on the possible outcomes. This should include some strong imagery[3] to assist in preventing negative thoughts.
3. Taking responsibility[4] for his actions whether they result in success or failure. Martin can then learn to take control of his game.
4. Building his self confidence.[5] For example, when practising Martin could pretend he was on the first tee and use his shot routine and relaxation trigger to overcome his fears. Every time he hits a good drive under the simulated pressure of the first tee he will experience success and his confidence will grow.

References:

1. pages 18–19
2. pages 51–54
3. page 28
4. pages 56–62
5. pages 65–67

14 BOB'S DREAM TURNS INTO A NIGHTMARE!

Bob was four up on Hugh, one of Dizzy Height's best players, in the final of the Club Championship. There were only eight holes to play and Hugh had just driven out of bounds on the eleventh. Surely Bob was going to win this hole and go five up with only seven holes left to play? This was what Bob had always dreamed of...beating Hugh in front of a big crowd to become the Club Champion. But to Bob, at that moment, it became his worst nightmare...*what if he was to follow Hugh out of bounds?...lose the hole...give Hugh confidence...start to play badly himself....*

It would be terrible to lose, I would never forget it... thought Bob. *I would have to live with the label of 'choker' for the rest of my life.*

What is happening in Bob's mind?

Bob is afraid of heights...

Bob is suffering from the 'fear of heights' syndrome where the fear is not usually about the elevation above ground level, but of the consequences of falling from that height. When Bob stood on the brink of his unexpected success, he was afraid of the consequences of failing to go on and win the match! When he realised the enormity of the occasion, he began to lose belief in himself, allowing negative thoughts to creep in.

What happened to Bob?

Bob had experienced this problem before and had worked on his mental skills to make him better prepared for this type of situation. However, this golden chance to become Club Champion was his biggest ever golfing moment, and he found it very difficult to stop the 'fear of failing' from taking hold in his mind. Just in time he managed to get back on track by bringing up his mental 'STOP' image.[1] He had practised bringing to mind a comical image of the rather bossy club president running across the green, face all red, yelling 'stop that, stop that'. This had the effect of stopping the torrent of negativity and making Bob chuckle.

Regaining some composure, he managed to remember to switch into his shot routine[2] and hit his tee shot. Although not very well struck, it came to rest in the light rough about 180 yards out. As he walked to the ball, he repeated some of his positive self-statements[3] like 'feeling good', 'enjoying this challenge'.

He made a scrappy one over par five, but still won the hole to go five up. Over the next few holes he used his relaxation trigger[4] to reduce his anxiety and tension. And, whenever the negative 'what if' thoughts returned, he was able to question them and develop a more positive and realistic thought. This gradually rebuilt his confidence. For example, when he had the thought: 'It will be terrible to lose, I'll never get over it', he strongly disputed it by saying, 'Hold on, am I just jumping to unnecessarily negative conclusions here?' He then countered with a more positive and realistic thought – 'For a start there is no reason why I should lose now and, even if I do, I will have still done well and I will get over the disappointment just as I have done before'.

Although Hugh, who was expecting Bob to choke, produced some birdies to reduce his deficit, a relieved Bob held on for victory on the seventeenth green. It had been a near thing, but Bob's mental skills had helped him achieve his dream. He knew he would be even stronger and more confident the next time he stood on the brink....

References:

1. pages 31–32
2. pages 51–53
3. pages 32–34
4. pages 18–19

15 THE LAST MINUTE DASH!

Tom had Saturday organised! The shopping had been done on Friday night; he had fixed the leaking tap during the week; and he had arranged for the family to have a day out with friends. He was free to get to the club in good time for his Medal round. He planned to have a coffee, then go to the practice range for half an hour followed by a session on the putting green. He would then have time for a relaxed lunch before his starting time at one o'clock.

Just as he was about to leave for the course, all hell broke loose! The friends phoned to say they couldn't come; his wife wanted to get some extra shopping she had forgotten the previous night; and the new kitten had gone missing!

Tom just made it to the first tee with seconds to spare. He was munching a chocolate bar as he hunted in his bag for some tees.

'You're first to play,' said his partner. So without even a practice swing Tom was on his way to one of his worst rounds ever.

What chance did I have? thought Tom to himself afterwards. *There was no way I could have found any rhythm or tempo today. My mind was going so fast I could never have calmed down and played a decent game.*

The vicious circle

Poor old Tom, you can really feel for him. He had done absolutely everything he possibly could to organise things so he would have plenty of time to prepare himself for the Medal – only to see his plans unravel in front of him. He felt powerless to do anything about events. He rushed round like a madman trying to pick up the pieces of his tattered plans, all the time thinking, 'This shouldn't be happening, why me?' As he ran around trying to get things done and realising he may be late, he felt ever more stressed.

When he finally rushed into the changing room and dragged on his golf shoes, fumbling with the laces and cursing under his breath, his head was spinning and his muscles were tense. He ran up to the first tee just in time. All he could think about was how uptight he felt and all the things that had gone wrong. He was still in 'hurry-up' mode as he teed off without even attempting his normal shot routine.

With his heart and mind racing, he rushed through his shots in a fraction of his usual time – rumour has it you can still see the scorched grass where Tom ran between shots! With heart, mind and body working at nineteen to the dozen, Tom had given himself no chance to get into his normal rhythm.

A plan for such emergencies

Well, this was one that Tom had to put down to experience. But it doesn't have to be that way. No matter how carefully we make our plans, the unexpected can happen, so it is worth having an emergency plan for such occasions. This is the plan we suggested to Tom:

1. First check your thinking and attitude[1] to what's happening. Remind yourself that, whilst you may have little control over some events, you do have control over the way you **react** to them. Tom would feel stressed when he demanded that things 'shouldn't be like this', so he now replaces that with 'it has happened, I have done all I can so **let it go**. I will concentrate my efforts on controlling the way I play golf.'

2. Develop a personal routine in the changing rooms, which you can

use for **every** game. When he is removing his shoes to get changed, Tom now imagines that all the thoughts and worries of the day are stuck to his shoes. So when he takes off the shoes and leaves them in the changing rooms **that is where he also leaves his everyday worries**. When he puts on his golf shoes, he puts on his golf thoughts! Incidentally, Tom does the reverse when taking off his golf shoes, even if he played badly he leaves those thoughts on the golf shoes, he tries never to let a bad game spoil his whole week!

3. When you have had to rush around to make your starting time and feel stressed, all those stress hormones rushing round your body tend to speed you up mentally and physically. You can sometimes go into a game almost not realising that you are in 'hurry-up' mode. It is very important to counteract this. When you start off too fast, it is very hard to slow down and find your natural rhythm and tempo – it just doesn't seem to be there any more! The solution is to try acting 'as-if' you are really relaxed and calm when you feel rushed or stressed. To help you do this, observe and learn from calm players, see what they do and how they move.

In fact, Tom watched a whole load of videos of one of his heroes Freddie Couples who, even in big tournaments, always manages to look like he is relaxing on holiday and just playing for fun! Tom practised mimicking Freddie: he 'walked the walk' and 'talked the talk', walking slowly and nonchalantly around the course grinning and enjoying the view. Strange as it might sound, if you feel anxious and stressed – **do not show it externally,** for example, by shaking your head, sighing, complaining etc. Instead, behave in a slow and calm fashion; if you 'act it', the feeling often follows!

You may have noticed that if you start slowly and gradually speed up, you are more likely to 'slot-in' to your rhythm; this may be because that is usually how we learn new skills, starting slowly and getting quicker as we get more proficient. So, if Tom arrives at the course feeling stressed, he just does his 'Freddie Couples' and starts his game in as slow and a relaxed manner as he can muster. By doing this he finds that after a few holes he starts to feel more relaxed and focused. He can then allow his rhythm to lift a little until it 'feels' he is back to his natural pace and tempo.

It is also helpful to regularly practise a relaxation technique away from the course and to develop a relaxation trigger[2] that will help you quickly release tension when needed.

Ultimately, the best advice we can give is to always plan, prepare and leave plenty of time for important games. But, unfortunately, as we all know: 'The best laid plans...' In which case, make sure you have a fallback strategy!

References:

1. pages 22–23
2. pages 18–19

16 JOHN'S PUTTING TOUCH DISAPPEARS!

John was one of the best putters in the club. He had a wonderful sense of touch and feel for judging long approach putts. If they didn't go in, they were hanging over the edge! John never gave much thought as to why he was such a good putter, apart from the fact that it saved him from paying out on many occasions! Then one day he seemed to lose his touch... He began to think how hard he had to hit the putt, whether it was uphill or downhill, was it longer than the one he had left short on the previous hole?

All of a sudden he couldn't get anywhere near the hole. His touch had gone. He knew he was now thinking about something that before he had done automatically. However, try as he might, he couldn't switch his mind off and his whole game deteriorated. What can John do to get his old putting touch back?

Don't interfere!

Poor old John. It is very easy to get lost in your thoughts, particularly if it is unfamiliar territory! Seriously though, this is a problem experienced by many golfers. So let's see what might be happening. As we discussed in the Basic Mental Skills section, golf is a game that requires very accurate control of a great number of muscles throughout the body. With practice, our brain learns how to control the minute muscle adjustments required to play a good shot or, as in John's case, to judge the pace and line of a long approach putt.

This control is so complex that we cannot describe in words how we do it – we just 'feel' it. If we try to take conscious control of such an action, one that has become automatic, then we interfere with it and it falls apart. Unfortunately, this is what has happened to John, his conscious attempt to control his putting stroke is now interfering with his natural movement.

Getting the 'feel' back

There are many skills in Chapter II that may be of use to John, but as for anyone, it is a question of experimenting to see what works best. To start with John should try:

▢ **Positive Self Talk**[1] Having realised what was happening, John tried to suppress the interfering thoughts. When he found he couldn't, he became distressed and angry, which affected his game even more. John could therefore devise some positive self-statements to remind himself that he is working on the problem. So, when he starts to have interfering thoughts, rather than get worked up he could repeat something like, 'There go those thoughts again. No big deal, I'm fixing the problem. I'll soon be waving them good-bye.'

▢ **Using a Relaxation Trigger**[2] The more relaxed we are, the less likely we are to be distracted by negative thoughts. Away from the golf course, John could create his own relaxation trigger, so that when he is about to putt he could use relaxing imagery to calm himself.

▢ **A new Putting Routine**[3] John should develop and practise a new putting routine and 'talk' himself through it every time. Most important of all, his routine needs to include a mental 'device' which will fill his conscious thoughts and block out the controlling thoughts as he putts. He will need to experiment to see what works best for him. Some people can hold their minds blank and concentrate on a spot on the ball. Other people have a 'swing thought' which they say in their heads. For John's problem he might try visualising a dustbin to putt into, or saying to himself, in a drawn out rhythmic way, 'roll ... it ... up'. This should help keep his putting stroke smooth.

References:

1. pages 32–34
2. pages 18–19
3. pages 51–54

17 HOW CAN I PLAY WITH ALL THIS NOISE?

'It's so hard to concentrate,' growled Jim, after duffing his chip into the bunker. 'How is anyone expected to play decently with all this chatter going on?' he continued, descending into the bunker. After three unsuccessful hacks at the ball – which was buried deep in the sand – Jim conceded the hole and stomped onto the next tee. 'You are too easily put off,' teased his partner. 'Those people were miles away. I couldn't hear them. You are just looking for excuses.'

You just don't understand... thought Jim. Without complete silence, Jim felt unable to concentrate fully on his shot. He heard even the smallest noises as he settled over the ball. Noises distracted him and prevented him keeping his mind on making a good swing. Jim was not looking for an excuse – he just wanted to be given what the etiquette of the game should allow him: silence in which to play his shot.

Although Jim would happily issue the butterflies with silencers and the birds with muzzles, total silence on every shot is clearly impossible. How, therefore, can Jim blot out these distractions and keep his mind on what he is doing?

Jim expects too much....

In many respects it is not difficult to have some sympathy for 'Unlucky' Jim. Excessive noise and distractions during a game can be a problem, but it does seem that he is rather oversensitive. Perhaps he could wear earplugs, but then he would be more sensitive to visual distractions so he would need to wear blinkers! Where would it all end?

Jim is a man who has very fixed ideas about the world. He holds very strong views on how people should behave, about manners and about 'right and wrong'. He holds very high standards for himself, but they are rigid, inflexible and the source of his difficulties. Because he holds these views, he believes that the rest of the world should also do the same. Unfortunately for Jim, the world, and other people are not as he would like, so he becomes angry and distressed.

On the golf course Jim would never walk across another player's line of sight or make any kind of sound that might disturb them. For Jim to play a decent golf shot there *must* be absolutely no distractions. If there isn't, in Jim's mind it simply becomes a prelude to disaster! So, when Jim tries to play his stroke and there is any kind of noise, because it goes against everything he believes, he becomes upset and angry, his body tenses and he is likely to duff the shot.

How Jim can learn to cope

Firstly, Jim could try being honest with himself. He is demanding that the world be the way he wants it to be, and failing to accept that it simply is not! What is more, he can't change it. He could start by changing his fixed and unhelpful attitudes[1] by asking himself, 'Does holding these attitudes help my game?' The answer is clearly 'No'. But remember, Jim holds his attitudes very strongly and it is difficult for him to accept that there could be a better attitude to adopt. To help, he could ask himself: 'Am I fretting about how I think things should be, instead of accepting them and dealing with them as they are?' and then reflect on his answer carefully.

To help him avoid such a strong emotional reaction when he hears a noise, he could develop some positive statements[2] to repeat to himself. The sort of thing that would help is, 'The world is full of noise which I can't control, so I can stop worrying about that', or 'I don't need silence to play good golf – any noise gives me a chance to practise and improve my concentration skills'.

It is also important that Jim makes sure he has developed a good set of shot routines[3] and that when he is carrying them out, he 'talks through' in his mind what he is doing. This will help him to focus on the task in hand and block out any distractions.

To hone his focusing skills[4] under actual conditions, Jim could try having a friend talk to him whilst he is practising, or go for a round on the local public course on a Sunday when it is at its busiest and noisiest!

References:

1. pages 22–23
2. pages 32–34
3. pages 51–54
4. pages 45–51

18
I DON'T DESERVE TO WIN...

Peter had only three holes to play in the Hilton Cup, he was level par and in line to win Dizzy Heights' premier stroke play competition. Suddenly his mind started telling him he didn't deserve to win, as he hadn't practised or worked at his game for nearly a year. *You don't deserve to win,* he told himself. *You only get out what you put in... You are lucky even to be in this position ... Your game won't hold up over these closing holes... Stand by, you are about to have a run of double bogeys...*

Peter is a scratch player and has won most of the club's major competitions several times, but hasn't won anything in the last few years because he's been concentrating on work and his family. He is convinced he can only enjoy success at the game if he is on the practice ground regularly. Is he right?

Peter's beliefs are challenged

Luckily for Peter his Scottish caddy Jock noticed that something was wrong, and asked him about it. Very confused, Peter expressed the thoughts in his mind.

'Dinna be so daft,' chided Jock. 'Are ye no jumping to conclusions?'

'Not at all,' came Peter's reply. 'It's inevitable. If I haven't done enough work I don't deserve to win, so I probably won't.'

Jock persisted. 'Have you ever thought this attitude might no be right?'

'What do you mean?'

'Well, if you've no done enough work or practice, then how come you've played so well for fifteen holes?'

'Luck?' replied Peter dubiously.

'Wid ye listen tae yersel! Nae other explanations?' Jock was getting exasperated.

'Well, maybe I have done enough practice over the years to carry me through,' responded Peter, a bit more hopefully.

'Of course ye have, and whit aboot all your efforts today?'

'You're right Jock, I have been working hard at focusing on the shots.'

Jock pressed on. 'And dae ye no think ye might be predicting the outcome a wee bit?'

'Yes. It sounds silly, doesn't it?'

'A guid player like yersel' should know better. Enough of this daft talk. Let's get back to work,' ordered Jock.

Peter felt his confidence returning and finished with three solid pars to lift the trophy.

Learning to question the old ways

This could be an example of 'golf imitating life'! Peter grew up in a home where everyone worked hard and all his family were high achievers. He learned at an early age that a good work ethic was important and there were rewards for those who worked. It was simple – 'If you worked hard, you were good, and fate would look after you; if you didn't, you were bad and deserved nothing'. Peter applied this belief to his entire life – including his golf. What is more, his golf seemed to provide the evidence that his belief was true; after all, he had worked hard at his golf and been very successful. But, on this occasion, he was brought to a standstill by the sudden realisation that here he was, doing really well, despite not having worked at his golf! Peter was experiencing something that flew in the face of everything he believed. The only way he could rationalise this paradox was to conclude that the round must end in disaster!

Jock's homespun philosophy was exactly what Peter required at that moment. Peter needs to question that long held belief[1] as it allowed him to be carried away by thoughts of outcomes and working obsessively towards distant goals. If he could change that rigid attitude he would probably find that his home-life and work would improve, as well, of course, as his golf! Perhaps it would then be a case of 'life imitating golf'!

References:

1. pages 22–23

19 WHO'S GOING TO COME SECOND?

It was a big day for Sue. Her recent good form had earned her a place in the County team, and here she was on the first tee being introduced to her opponent, Tessa. Tessa was much older than Sue, and had been a dominant figure in women's golf in the area for many years. Tessa exuded confidence and self-assurance. Sue thought Tessa's bag was bigger than hers, her clubs were newer, the spikes on her shoes looked longer and sharper! Tessa's whole attitude seemed to convey the message, 'I am better than you, and I am going to beat you.'

'First game then?' asked Tessa in a menacing tone.

'Yes. I'm a bit nervous. I hope I can give you some sort of a game,' replied Sue, who by now was completely intimidated and mentally pre-pared for defeat. *If I lose by only 5 and 4 I will be happy*, she thought to herself.

'When I was your age I worked much harder on my short game than you appear to have done,' observed Tessa acidly as they shook hands on the twelfth green. Sue had managed to win a couple of holes! 'You could be good enough to give me a close game if you practised more,' advised Tessa. *You arrogant so and so . . .* thought Sue, relieved that it was all over.

When she was recounting the match to her pals back at Dizzy Heights the next day, Sue realised that she had allowed herself to be intimidated by Tessa. She had felt mentally beaten before she had even started!

How could Sue have avoided Tessa getting the upper hand mentally?

Don't talk yourself down...

Sue could see how she had been mentally beaten and understood what had happened. She had talked herself into defeat by talking down her ability both to her opponent and to herself! Unfortunately, it was a pattern she had been all too familiar with throughout her life. Her parents had taught her to be modest; they said that appearing 'confident' and 'being full of yourself' was just arrogance and would make her unpopular.

Now compare that attitude to Tessa's approach. Tessa had always been pretty confident, but had built on her confidence after years of experience and success. That experience had also taught her some 'gamesmanship', and she new that acting very confidently and playing on any of her opponent's psychological weaknesses would give her an advantage. She knew that, in matches where players were of similar technical skill, superior mental skills would always be the deciding factor.

Sue realised that Tessa's ploy only worked because she fell for it! You can't stop your opponent using gamesmanship, but you can neutralise it, or even turn it to your advantage, with your own good mental skills.

Sue takes a new approach

Sue knew she needed to change, but was stuck on how to do it until she read the 'Getting your Thinking Right'[1] section of *Golf Between the Ears*. She started to question the old beliefs she held by asking herself – 'Has this over modest and self-effacing attitude always worked for me, in my life let alone my golf?' 'Is being justifiably proud and confident of my achievements **really** arrogance?' The answer appeared to be a resounding 'no' as there is plenty of evidence that many people who are competent, quietly confident and believe in themselves are also popular; very popular, in fact, because they are inspiring and reassuring for others around them! From that point on, Sue started to believe that it was okay to feel good about herself.

Sue then read the section on 'Building Confidence' and developed positive self-statements[2] reminding herself that she worked hard at her golf and deserved her success and achievements. She also removed all 'put-downs' and self-criticism from her thoughts and conversation.

She borrowed some videotapes showing top female golfers and sportswomen. Sue watched them carefully to learn how to look controlled and confident. From these she learned how to walk and stand in a confident and relaxed manner, with an unconcerned look and her head slightly up. With the help of her sister (and squeezing a tennis ball to increase wrist strength) she practised developing a firm handshake. A friend who taught communication and presentation skills showed her how to look confident by holding steady eye contact with another person. Sue found this hard at first, but learned the trick of looking at the other person's eyebrows, which felt easier but still appears to be direct eye contact.

As Sue developed these skills and acted 'as-if'[3] she were confident, she started to genuinely **feel** more confident. In fact, the following season, she found herself up against Terrible Tessa again. When they met up on the way to the first tee, Tessa boomed at Sue, 'Ah, yes, I remember it was over pretty quickly the last time we played. Hope you can make a better game of it this time'. The old Sue would have felt dreadful, and apologised and stammered something about doing her best, but couldn't promise anything! However this time it was different! Sue gave Tessa a good firm handshake and smiled in a relaxed and confident manner.

Looking her opponent straight in the eye she said, 'Hello Tessa, it's nice to be playing you again. You're right, **you** won last time and I learned such a lot from that match. I'm really looking forward to our game today. Right, now let's get on with it – your honour, I believe!'

Tessa was visibly surprised that Sue seemed unashamed about the last match and now appeared confident and undaunted. Tessa's psychological games no longer worked on Sue.

We can report that the game was very close indeed...

References:

1. pages 20–38
2. pages 32–34
3. pages 65–67

20
I MIGHT NEVER LIVE THIS DOWN

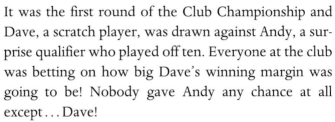

It was the first round of the Club Championship and Dave, a scratch player, was drawn against Andy, a surprise qualifier who played off ten. Everyone at the club was betting on how big Dave's winning margin was going to be! Nobody gave Andy any chance at all except...Dave!

As they were called to the first tee, the thoughts raced through Dave's head... *What if I get off to a bad start?...What if he starts well and becomes confident?...He has nothing to lose...There is no pressure on him...I am on a hiding to nothing...If I win it was a foregone conclusion, but if I lose I will never live it down...*

Dave had been in this situation before and had managed to win by the narrowest of margins. He knew his mental approach was poor and that one day it would lead to the defeat he didn't want to contemplate...

Winning can be too important

Winning is everything to Dave. He always recalled his old Dad saying to him, 'No one ever remembers who came second! There is no point doing anything unless you win and be seen to win.' Dave applied this to everything in his life and golf was no exception. He drove himself relentlessly to be the best golfer – to win at all cost. In every game he focused only on the thought of winning. If he won a game he would feel okay, although he always felt he should have won by more, or that maybe because his opponent was not playing so well his victory didn't look so good – victory was always a little disappointing. But, it sure as hell beat losing! When he lost, Dave would feel devastated. In fact he would often feel bad all the following week.

The importance Dave places on winning is holding him back from achieving his full potential, because he introduces the fear of losing into his thoughts. He needs some help to get his thinking on the right lines and, just in time, he gets the advice he needs from a most unexpected source . . .

Joe has the answer!

As he morosely dragged his trolley towards the first tee, he was so lost in his thoughts that he walked right into someone. It was the wizened figure of the man known to everybody in the club as 'Joe 19'. No one was quite sure if they had ever seen Joe play a round of golf, he was just part of the furniture – the bar furniture that is! There were rumours that many years ago Joe had been a talented young professional whose career had been cut short by some 'tragedy'.

'Steady on, Sonny,' the old man growled.

Dave almost smiled, middle-aged men don't often get called 'Sonny'.

'Sorry, Joe, my mind was elsewhere.'

'Yeah, no doubt thinking about how humiliating it will be to get beaten by a young player with a ten handicap. You'd be laughed out of the club.'

Dave winced. 'Thanks for your support, Joe!'

The old man was unperturbed 'That's okay. I saw you when you nearly blew it against that eight handicapper in last year's championship. I don't think you hit one straight shot – spent more time in the rough than a frightened grass snake. In fact, I'll wager with you that you won't hit more than eight greens in regulation today!'

Dave was appalled that anyone could suggest a scratch golfer could-n't achieve that. 'You're on, Joe. I'll make you eat your words you cheeky...!'

Dave strode up to the first tee, hardly noticing his opponent Andy. He had made up his mind to prove old Joe wrong and focused on getting all his tee shots on the fairway. Dave knew that he needed to stay relaxed, like in a practice round, keep a nice easy tempo and pick comfortable achievable targets like the middle of the green for his approach shots. He felt the tension fall away as he teed of. As the round progressed, he chatted to Andy in between shots and even offered him some good tips.

Both men played well, but Dave won the match comfortably as many had predicted. Within himself, Dave was pleased to have won, but more importantly he thought to himself, *I've won the bet.* He couldn't wait to see Joe.

Sure enough, back at the clubhouse, there was Joe, propped up at the bar. 'How did it go then? Guess I lost the bet.'

'You sure did. I hit every green except one in regulation.'

'Did you win the match?'

'Of course I did, the way I was playing.'

'Were you not the one who was worried about losing?'

'Well, yes. That's what I don't quite understand, Joe. I won comfortably, but during the game I didn't try to win. I hardly gave a thought to "winning".'

Joe nodded wisely. 'What were you thinking about then?'

'Well, I just focused on making each shot a good accurate one – so I could prove you wrong.'

'Exactly. If you set winning as your only goal[1] for the game, you will worry about the consequences of losing, which you judged as very high in this case. That's all there was to be had from the game – not much, huh? The pressure you put on yourself to not lose is then intense, with little motivation to win – a recipe for poor playing. But when you focused on the quality of each individual shot, you had plenty to gain from the satisfaction of staying on target. After a few holes you were achieving your goals, which gave you a sense of confidence and enjoyment. You stayed relaxed and so played to the best of your ability. The result took care of itself!'

'You crafty old blighter, you knew exactly what you were doing when you made that wager with me. I may have won the bet, but I would like to treat you. What can I get you?'

'Well, since you're offering, you could pick up my bar tab for today.'

Dave coughed. 'Er...well, I wasn't really thinking of spending quite such a large amount, Joe!'

References:

1. pages 39–44

Appendix

Creating your own relaxation technique for golf

The first step is to record the following script onto a blank tape using your own voice, leaving pauses as shown. Make the length of the pauses what feels right for you. If you think someone else's voice would be more relaxing, get them to record the script! As you get towards the end of the script you should be speaking quieter and slower than you were at the beginning, to reflect the relaxed feeling.

The Script
[start here]

As you do this exercise, if you get any strange feelings such as a tingling sensation, light headedness or a feeling of 'floating' perhaps, do not be alarmed as this is quite normal. If you feel distressed or uncomfortable with these feelings at any time, you can open your eyes and the feelings will go away. If you carry on with the relaxation exercise, usually the feelings will disappear anyway.

Make yourself as comfortable as possible in a reasonably upright position so you are less likely to fall asleep!
Allow your eyes to slowly and gently close

[Pause]

Listen to the sounds that you can hear around you

[Long pause]

Now try to listen to each sound one at a time for about 5 to 10 seconds each

[Long Pause]

Now listen to all the sounds together

[Pause]

You will be aware that these sounds will come and go through the session and you can choose to let them just drift through your mind or choose to ignore them

[Pause]

Making sure your eyelids stay gently closed and without moving your head, roll your eyes upwards as if you are looking up towards the top of your head

[Long pause]

As you do this for a while notice how heavy and tired your eyes become

[Pause]

Feel the heaviness in the muscles of your eyes

[Pause]

And as this feeling gets very heavy just allow your eyes to drop down

[Pause]

Now notice the feeling of tiredness and relaxation in your eyes

[Pause]

Let that heavy relaxed feeling roll down your face to your mouth and jaw

[Pause]

Allow the heaviness to relax your jaw

[Pause]

Now feel that heavy relaxed feeling in your tongue and face

[Pause]

Now let that heavy relaxed feeling in your eyes roll over your head

[Pause]

Pushing away the tightness and tension in your head

[Long pause]

Now feel that relaxation roll down the back of your head

[Pause]

Down through your neck

[Pause]

Down into your shoulders

[Pause]

Allow your shoulders to relax, feel them drop down

[Long pause]

Allow that relaxed heavy feeling in your shoulders to roll slowly down through your arms. Allow that heavy feeling to roll right down into your fingers

[Pause]

And as that heavy relaxed feeling rolls through your arms, feel a comforting warmth flow through to your fingers

[Long Pause]

Now allow that relaxed heavy feeling to roll down through your body

[Pause]

Feel that relaxed heavy feeling roll down through your chest

[Pause]

Down through your stomach

[Pause]

Down through your back

[Pause]

Now allow yourself to become aware of the heavy and warm feeling through your body

[Long pause]

Now let that warm heavy relaxed feeling roll down from your body through in to your legs

[Pause]

Down through your thighs

[Pause]

Down through your knees
[Pause]
And now let that heavy warm relaxed feeling roll down through your ankles down in to your toes
[Pause]
Now feel how warm and heavy and relaxed your legs have become
[Long pause]
Now be aware that the heavy warm feeling of relaxation fills your body and replaces the tension that was there before
[Long pause]
Now I want you to think of your **favourite relaxing image** of somewhere, real or imaginary, where you will feel happy and relaxed
[Pause]
Picture it clearly in your mind
[Pause]
Notice all the things there are to see
[Long pause]
Look at all the shapes and all the colours
[Pause]
Become aware of any pleasant smell
[Pause]
Become aware of any sounds
[Pause]
Notice anything that you can feel, perhaps the wind or perhaps you can reach out and touch something
[Pause]
Notice how relaxed you feel when you hold this image in your mind
[Long pause]
In the future, maybe on the golf course and you need to relax, whenever you bring your favourite relaxing image to mind you will remember this relaxed warm feeling you have now and feel it again at that moment
[Long pause]

Just check your body again and take a few moments to notice that heavy, warm relaxed feeling

[Pause]

Now pay attention to your breathing and notice it going in and out

[Pause]

Now as you breathe out say the word 'calm' in your mind

[Pause]

As you are doing this you may be aware of stray thoughts entering your mind. This does not matter at all. You don't have to engage with them. Imagine they are just clouds that blow through your mind. Just wave them 'goodbye' as they pass through

[Pause]

Just bring your mind back to repeating 'calm' slowly each time you breathe out

[Long pause]

As you repeat the word 'calm' each time you breathe out become aware of how relaxed you feel

[Pause]

Now whenever you need to feel more relaxed, perhaps on the golf course and about to play an important shot, by focusing on your breathing and repeating the word 'calm' as you breathe out you will be able to remember this feeling of relaxation

[Pause]

In a moment I am going to count back down from 10, and as I do you will become more and more aware of your surroundings. As I get to 1 you will slowly open your eyes and readjust to what is around you. You will still feel relaxed but fully alert. You will also remember how you can quickly recreate this feeling of relaxation and alertness even on the golf course

[Pause]

10 . . . 9 . . . 8 . . . 7 . . . 6 . . .

You can feel yourself becoming more aware of your surroundings

5 . . . 4 . . . 3 . . . 2 . . . 1

Now you may slowly open your eyes and feel alert and refreshed but still relaxed.

[the end]

Once the above script has been recorded, then get yourself settled in a comfortable, upright chair and play the tape back to yourself regularly. We cannot emphasise enough that this technique must be practised as often as possible, particularly at the outset. The objective is to make you associate either:

repeating the word 'calm' as you breathe out
or
your relaxing image

with a feeling of physical relaxation and lack of tension. So if, for example, you are facing up to a vital putt and you start to feel yourself tense up, then by using your relaxing image or breathing slowly and repeating the word 'calm' on exhalation you can bring about rapid relief from tension. Clearly, the more often you practise this technique the better control you will have over your tension during a game.

This is only one of many relaxation techniques, and it may be worthwhile investigating others to find the particular technique that best suits you.

Acknowledgements

Our sincere thanks are due to all the people we have met in the world of golf who have helped, through their experience and friendship, to make this book possible. We are particularly grateful to John Raymond and Iain MacInnes for their suggestions and advice. Regretfully, the others are too numerous to mention individually, but you will all know who you are! We look forward to meeting you again on and off the fairway!

To get all the latest news from the **Dizzy Heights Golf Club** visit the *Golf Between the Ears* website at:

www.golfbte.co.uk